THE POLITICAL THEORY OF BOLSHEVISM

A Critical Analysis

BY

HANS KELSEN

THE LAWBOOK EXCHANGE, LTD.
Clark, New Jersey

ISBN 9781584777649 (hardcover)
ISBN 9781616191610 (paperback)

Lawbook Exchange edition 2007, 2011

Reprinted with permission from the Hans Kelsen-Institut

The quality of this reprint is equivalent to the quality of the original work.

THE LAWBOOK EXCHANGE, LTD.
33 Terminal Avenue
Clark, New Jersey 07066-1321

*Please see our website for a selection of our other publications
and fine facsimile reprints of classic works of legal history:*
www.lawbookexchange.com

Library of Congress Cataloging-in-Publication Data

Kelsen, Hans, 1881-1973.
  The political theory of Bolshevism : a critical analysis / Hans
Kelsen.
      p. cm.
  Originally published: Berkeley : University of California Press,
1948.
  Includes bibliographical references.
  ISBN-13: 978-1-58477-764-9 (cloth : alk. paper)
  ISBN-10: 1-58477-764-8 (cloth : alk. paper)
  1. Communism. 2. State, The. I. Title.
  HX72.K45 2007
  320.53'22--dc22

                              2006034314

Printed in the United States of America on acid-free paper

THE POLITICAL THEORY
OF BOLSHEVISM

A Critical Analysis

BY

HANS KELSEN

UNIVERSITY OF CALIFORNIA PRESS
BERKELEY AND LOS ANGELES
1948

University of California Publications in Political Science

Editors (Los Angeles): M. W. Graham, R. H. Fitzgibbon, F. M. Stewart

Volume 2, No. 1, pp. 1–60

Submitted by editors February 13, 1948
Issued September 28, 1948
Price, $1.00

University of California Press
Berkeley and Los Angeles
California

❖

Cambridge University Press
London, England

CONTENTS

Contents

INTRODUCTION

THE ASSOCIATION of the Soviet Union and the Western Powers, imposed upon them by the Charter of the United Nations, has created the problem of whether, in view of the difference in the respective political systems, coöperation is possible between them within a relatively centralized international organization. Those who rightly consider such coöperation as a fundamental condition of world peace sometimes try to veil the basic difficulty by asserting that the difference concerned is not essential. Both political systems, that of the Soviet Union and that of the Western Powers, they say, are democracies; the Soviet system merely represents a new form of democracy. Some people even go so far as to contend that the Soviet government is a better and more perfect type of democracy, since—in contradistinction to the capitalistic democracies—it guarantees social security.

The Soviet regime is more than any other political system connected with a political ideology which it uses as an intellectual instrument for its justification; and no other regime needs more urgently a justification than the totalitarian dictatorship of Bolshevism. Its ideology is the social philosophy of Marx and Engels as interpreted by Lenin and Stalin. The center of this philosophy is a political theory according to which the state as a coercive order is necessary only for the maintenance of capitalistic exploitation and, consequently, will disappear when socialism is established. Marx and Engels predicted the disappearance of the coercive order as the automatic effect of the establishment of socialism within a single state. Since this prediction evidently did not come true in Soviet Russia, Lenin and Stalin were forced to modify the original doctrine by postponing the disappearance of the state to the time when socialism will be realized all over the world. According to the new doctrine it is only the socialist world state which can and will disappear. Since this event is not to be expected in the near future, the provisional character of the coercive machinery maintained in the Soviet Union needs all the more to be emphasized. For as a mere transitory stage on the way to a free society even a totalitarian state may be considered by the people as endurable, especially if its dictatorship is interpreted as democracy.

The purpose of this study is to show the paradoxical contradiction which exists within Bolshevism between anarchism in theory and totalitarianism in practice, and to defend the true idea of democracy against the attempt to obliterate and to adulterate it by presenting a party dictatorship as the political self-determination of a free people. Particular stress is laid upon the proof that the slogan of the two democracies—a formal-political and a substantive-economic one—is wrong. There is here much more than a terminological quarrel. The relationship between democracy and socialism is at stake. The Russian attempt to establish socialism by revolution and the dictatorship of a Communist party has found its rival in the enterprise of the English people to attain the same goal in the way of evolution and under true democracy in the traditional sense of the term. The interpretation of democracy thus implies the decision between two basically different processes, on which, perhaps, the fate of mankind will depend.

Part One

ANARCHISM OR TOTALITARIANISM

ANARCHISM OR TOTALITARIANISM

CONCEPT OF THE STATE

THE THEORY OF THE State involves two different problems and, consequently, requires two different disciplines. One approach considers the state as a phenomenon of social reality: the state as it actually is, the historical state; the other considers the state as an object of valuation: the state as it ought, or ought not, to be, the just and unjust state. From the point of view of the first-mentioned discipline, we may ask: what is *the state?* What is its essence, its origin, its structure, and what are its essential functions? These questions can be answered on the basis of a comparative study of the social phenomena called *state,* although states are very different in different historical periods and in different geographical areas.

As the result of such a study the state may be defined as a social order, that is, a set of rules regulating the mutual behavior of individuals, an order which is characterized by the following elements: it is a coercive order, that is to say, it tries to bring about the desired human behavior by providing coercive acts as sanctions for the contrary behavior. That means that this order is a legal order. It is a relatively centralized order. It institutes special organs for the creation and application of its rules, especially a centralized executive power at the disposal of an organ which has the character of a government. This government must be independent, and the coercive order applied by it must be effective for a definite territory.

It is usual to characterize the state as a community rather than as an order. But the state as a community is constituted by "its" coercive order and is not an entity different from this order. It is usual also to personify the community, or the order constituting it, and to speak of it as of an acting person. But the state acts only through those individuals who have the character of organs. These are the individuals authorized by the order to create and apply its rules.

RESTRICTION OF FREEDOM

Since every social order regulating the mutual behavior of individuals, and especially a coercive order, inevitably constitutes a restriction of freedom—and freedom is considered a fundamental value in social life—it is usual to distinguish the coercive orders we call states according to the degree to which they restrict the freedom of the individuals subjected to them. There are two different criteria according to which the restriction of individual freedom by the state order may be judged: the way in which the rules of the state order are created and applied; and the scope of the state order, that is to say, the extent to which the rules of the order regulate human life. The restriction of individual freedom is at its minimum and the degree of individual freedom is at its maximum if: one, the rules of the coercive order are created and applied by those whose behavior is regulated by the order (autonomy); two, if the scope of the coercive order is as limited as possible, so that the mutual behavior of the individuals is regulated only so far as is necessary to protect certain vital interests, such as life and property (liberalism). The restriction of individual freedom is at its maximum and the degree of individual freedom at its minimum if: one, those who are subjected to the order are excluded from its creation and application and these functions are reserved to a single individual or to a relatively small group of individuals, legally or actually not subjected to the order (heteronomy); and, two, if the scope of the coercive order is in principle unlimited, so that the mutual behavior of the individuals is regulated in every possible aspect of human life, especially with respect to economic and cultural life (étatism or totalitarianism). Nationalization of economic production, the quintessence of state socialism, is the characteristic measure of expanding the scope of a state order toward totalitarianism.

Concept of Democracy

The two criteria: the way in which the state order is created and applied, and the scope of the state order, need not necessarily be combined. For, the first refers to the form of the state, the second to its content; and the differentiation between form and content serves in the first place to express the mutual independence of the two criteria. A state order may correspond to the principle of autonomy and, at the same time, have a totalitarian character; and a state order may have a heteronomous character and, at the same time, its scope may correspond to the principle of liberalism. The traditional distinction of two basic forms of government: democracy and autocracy, refers, in the main (but not only), to the first of the two criteria, the way in which the state order is created and applied, to the *form* of the state; the distinction also refers to a certain extent to the second: the *scope* of the state order as it affects the content of the state. A state is a democracy if the legislative and executive powers are exercised by the people either directly in a popular assembly, or indirectly by organs elected by the people on the basis of universal and equal suffrage. Since the highest degree of autonomy, the requirement of unanimity for the creation and application of the order, is equivalent to anarchy, the principle of majority decisions in collegiate organs represents the maximum of autonomy possible within a social order. It is an essential element of the form of government called democracy, which is the political realization of the principle of autonomy or self-determination.

Although this principle is quite compatible with liberalism as well as with étatism—a democracy may be a liberal-capitalist, a socialist, and even a totalitarian, state, just as an autocracy may have a liberal or totalitarian character—the usual concept of democracy includes, as an element essential to this form of government, certain limitations of the legislative and executive power of the state. For a state to be democratic it is not sufficient that the citizens thereof should participate directly or indirectly in the formation of the will of the state; in addition the constitution must guarantee to the citizens freedom of conscience, of speech, the press and, especially, freedom of association. The formation of political parties and their participation in the political life of the nation, especially in election of the organs of the state, must not be limited or prevented by legislative or executive acts. The legal and actual possibility of more than one political party is so vital a condition of democracy that a one-party state, even if its constitution should fulfill all the other requirements of democracy, is much more remote from the latter type of government than a state whose constitution restricts the right of voting to a minority of the population. Democracy, according to the generally accepted meaning of the term, requires that the idea of freedom be realized not only positively, that is to say, in the direct or indirect participation in government of all citizens, but also negatively, that is to say, by granting the essential freedoms, among which the freedom of political parties is the most important one. Autocracy, on the other hand, is characterized not only by the fact that the mass of the people is excluded from any participation in government, but also by the absence of the essential freedoms, especially freedom of political parties. The modern type of autocracy—which in former times appeared under the names of tyranny, despotism, absolute monarchy—is the party dictatorship.

THEORY OF POLITICS AND "POLITICAL" THEORY

The analysis of the various forms of the state order, especially of the forms of government such as democracy and autocracy, and the examination of the typical content of the state order, especially of the principles of liberalism and étatism, is the task of a political theory as a science of the state. So far as this discipline is strictly confined to describing, classifying, and explaining the mentioned phenomena in the same way as natural science deals with plants or animals, it has the character of a pure science. Like the natural scientist, the political scientist, the theorist of the state, looks at the object of his science from outside, and registers impartially what he sees as though he were not personally concerned. His statements do not imply any value judgments concerning democracy and autocracy, liberalism and étatism. It is not the task of a scientific theory of the state to determine whether a particular form of the state or a particular scope of the state order is good or bad. It is, instead, the function of a true science of the state to analyze, to understand, and to explain the form or scope of the state order. Value judgments, in contradistinction to statements about reality, have a purely subjective character. They are based on our wishes and fears, that is to say, on the emotional element of our consciousness. They are valid only for the judging subject, for they are not verifiable by facts. In this respect they differ essentially from the objective statements by which reality is described and explained, statements which are based on the rational element of our consciousness. Evaluation is certainly an essential condition of action. No action is possible without previous evaluation. But action represents an attitude totally different from scientific description and explanation. Action is the very core of politics. But to preserve its objective character, science must be separated from politics; and this can be done only by eliminating any subjective value judgment from science; especially from the science of the state as a phenomenon of politics. The science of the state is a "political" theory only so far as it has a political phenomenon for its object. This is possible without misusing an allegedly scientific theory of the state as a means of politics. The theory of the state gives up its character as a science and becomes part of a political activity if, instead of describing and explaining the state as a phenomenon of social reality, it renders value judgments concerning the state. The questions concerning the value of the state as such and of its various forms and contents must be determined by a discipline which, not partaking of the character of a science, is a political theory in the specific sense of the term.

VALUE OF THE STATE

Since these questions aim at value judgments, which by their very nature have a subjective character, it is not astonishing that there is no agreement among political thinkers on these questions—there never was and never will be agreement. There are and always have been thinkers who maintain that the state is the highest good and an absolute necessity for civilization; and there are others who declare the state an evil, the social evil *par excellence,* and who, consequently, demand its abolition and replacement by a free, that is stateless, society. The latter view is the doctrine of anarchism.

ÉTATISM : HEGEL

A very characteristic protagonist of the doctrine which advocates a radical étatism was the German philosopher Hegel. His interpretation of history results in a deification of the state. According to his philosophy,[1] all that exists is rational (the "Real is the Rational"), but the state is "absolutely rational." It is the "realized ethical idea or ethical spirit." It results from the nature of the state "that it has the highest right over the individual whose highest duty in turn is to be a member of the state"; a membership which implies unconditional obedience toward the established authority of the state. The individual, says Hegel, exists only through the state; "he has his truth, real existence and ethical

---

[1] G. W. F. Hegel, *Philosophy of Right,* trans. by S. W. Dyde (London, 1896) §§257, 258.

status only as being a member of the state." According to a religious view of the world, nature is a manifestation of God; but according to Hegel, the state is the conscious manifestation of God. Nature is only an unconscious, and, therefore, incomplete manifestation. "The state is the spirit which abides in the world and there realizes itself consciously; while in nature it is realized only as the other of itself or the sleeping spirit. Only when it [the divine spirit] is present in consciousness, knowing itself as an existing object, it is the state."[2] From a rationalistic point of view, the state exists only in the mind of the individuals who adapt their behavior to the social order we call the state, which is not a real entity as are physical things. According to Hegel, however, the state has even more objective reality than physical nature, for it is a realization of the absolute spirit in the realm of consciousness. Hegel says: "The state is the march of God in the world; its ground or cause is the power of reason realizing itself as will." Every state, whatever it be, participates in the divine essence of the idea, "this actual God." "The state is not a work of art"; only divine reason could produce it. "The nation as a state is the (divine) spirit substantively realized and directly real. Hence it is the absolute power on earth."[3] This means: the state is God on earth.

ANARCHISM : MARX AND ENGELS

Other thinkers, for example, the Frenchman Pierre Joseph Proudhon, the Russians Michael Alexandrovich Bakunin and Peter Alexevich Kropotkin, the great Leo Tolstoi, answer the question of the value of the state in a negative sense. They are representatives of that theoretical anarchism which proclaims that the coercive order of the state is the source of most, if not of all, social evils, and a free, that is, stateless, society is possible and desirable. It is highly significant that the most important of all anarchistic doctrines has been developed on a philosophical basis which is only a slight modification of Hegel's philosophy of history, by a pupil of Hegel, namely Karl Marx. According to the doctrine of Marx and his friend Friedrich Engels,[4] the state is by its very nature a coercive machinery whose function is to maintain

---

[2] *Ibid.*, §258.
[3] *Ibid.*, §331.
[4] Hans Kelsen, *Sozialismus und Staat. Eine Untersuchung der politischen Theorie des Marxismus.* 2. Aufl. (Leipzig, 1923).

the domination of one group—the group of individuals in possession of the means of production, the class of the capitalists—over another group formed by those who do not participate in the ownership of the goods called capital, the class of the exploited proletariat. The state is a coercive organization for the purpose of maintaining the suppression of one class by another. By the revolutionary establishment of socialism, that is by the abolition of private property in, and the socialization of, the means of production, the system of capitalism, and with it the state, as a social institution, will disappear. The state will "wither away." The socialist society of the future will be a stateless society, a society the order of which will be maintained without the employment of force. This will be possible since the social order will naturally be in the interest of everybody, so that nobody will be induced to violate the order. But this ideal condition of mankind cannot be established immediately after the socialist revolution has abolished capitalism. Between the capitalist state and the communist stateless society there will be an intermediate stage, the dictatorship of the proletariat, which is the immediate result of the proletarian revolution. The dictatorship of the proletariat will be a state with a true government and will differ from the capitalist state only so far as the purpose of this coercive machinery will be not to maintain, but to destroy the exploitation of one class by another.

In his book *The Origin of the Family, Private Property and the State* Engels says:

The state is therefore by no means a power imposed on society from without; just as little is it "the reality of the moral idea, the image and reality of reason," as Hegel maintains. Rather it is a product of society at a particular stage of development; it is the admission that this society has involved itself in insoluble self-contradiction and is cleft into irreconcilable antagonisms which it is powerless to exorcise. But in order that these antagonisms, classes with conflicting economic interests, shall not consume themselves and society in fruitless struggle, a power, apparently standing above society, has become necessary to moderate the conflict and keep it within the bounds of "order"; and this power, arisen out of society, but placing itself above it and increasingly alienating itself from it, is the state. . . . As the state arose from the need to keep class antagonisms in check, but also arose in the thick of the fight between the classes, it is normally the state of the most powerful economically ruling class, which by its means becomes also the politically ruling class, and so acquires new means of holding down and exploiting the oppressed class.[5]

---

[5] Marxist Library, Vol. XXII (New York, 1942), pp. 155 ff.

In his book *Anti-Dühring,* Engels describes the way in which the state will disappear:

The proletariat seizes state power, and then transforms the means of production into state property. But in doing this, it puts an end to itself as the proletariat, it puts an end to all class differences and class antagonisms, it puts an end also to the state as the state. Former society, moving in class antagonism, had need of the state, that is an organization of the exploiting class at each period for the maintenance of its external conditions of production ... As soon as there is no longer any class of society to be held in subjection; as soon as, along with class domination and the struggle for individual existence based on the former anarchy of production, the collisions and excesses arising from these have also been abolished, there is nothing more to be repressed, and a special repressive force, a state, is no longer necessary. The first act in which the state really comes forward as the representative of society as a whole— the seizure of the means of production in the name of society—is at the same time its last independent act as a state. The interference of a state power in social relations becomes superfluous in one sphere after another, and then becomes dormant of itself. Government over persons is replaced by the administration of things and the direction of the processes of production. The state is not "abolished," it withers away. It is from this standpoint that we must appraise the phrase "people's free state" [a slogan of the German Social Democrat party]—both its justification at times for agitational purposes, and its ultimate scientific inadequacy—and also the demand of the so-called Anarchists that the state should be abolished over night.[9]

The difference between the Marxian political theorists and the so-called Anarchists is only that the latter demand the abolishment of the state by a revolutionary action, whereas the former predict an automatic disappearance of the state after the dictatorship of the proletariat, the proletarian state, has been established by the socialist revolution. So far as the social ideal is concerned Marxism is anarchism.

Finally, there appears in Engels' *Origin of the Family, Private Property and the State* the often-quoted statement:

The state, therefore, has not existed from all eternity. There have been societies which have managed without it, which had no notion of the state or state power. At a definite stage of economic development, which necessarily involved the cleavage of society into classes, the state became a necessity because of this cleavage. We are now rapidly approaching a stage in the development of production at which the existence of these classes has not only ceased to be a necessity, but becomes a positive hindrance to production. They will fall as inevitably as they once arose. The state inevitably falls with them.

[9] *Idem, Herr Eugen Dühring's Revolution in Science* [*Anti-Dühring*] (New York, 1939), pp. 306 ff.

The society which organizes production anew on the basis of free and equal association of the producers will put the whole state machinery where it will then belong—into the museum of antiquities, next to the spinning wheel and the bronze ax.[7]

BOLSHEVISM : LENIN

This doctrine is the official political ideology of Bolshevism. In the socialist literature of the end of the nineteenth century, and the beginning of the twentieth, the Marxian theory of the state, especially its revolutionary tendency and its ultimate goal of an anarchic society, was more or less ignored or obliterated. The most important socialist party on the European continent, the German Social Democratic, in spite of its acceptance of the Marxian doctrine, adhered to an evolutionary, rather than a revolutionary, policy. It was against this "adulteration of Marxism" that V. I. Lenin published his famous pamphlet *State and Revolution* in 1917. He accused the "opportunists within the Labor movement" of attempting to "obliterate and distort the revolutionary side of Marx's teaching, its revolutionary soul." The purpose of his pamphlet was "to resuscitate the real teachings of Marx on the state."[8] The reëstablished Marxian doctrine of the state as interpreted by Lenin has been incorporated in the "Program of the Communist International,"[9] an organization which was hardly more than an instrument of the Russian Bolshevik party and was active until its formal dissolution in 1943. Its program reflected the Bolshevik doctrine of the state. It contains the following statements: "The state, being the embodiment of class domination, will die out, insofar as classes die out, and with it all measures of coercion will expire." But "Between the capitalist society and communist society a period of revolutionary transformation intervenes, during which the one changes into the other. Correspondingly, there is also an intervening period of political transition in which the essential state form is the revolutionary dictatorship of the proletariat." "The characteristic feature of the transition

---

[7] *Idem, loc. cit.*

[8] V. I. Lenin, *State and Revolution.* Little Lenin Library, vol. 14 (New York, 1935), p. 7.

[9] In: *Blueprint for World Conquest, as outlined by the Communist International.* With an introduction by William Henry Chamberlin. Human Events (Washington, D.C., and Chicago, 1946), pp. 149 ff. The passages quoted above are taken from the program as adopted by the Sixth World Congress, September 1, 1928, in Moscow.

period as a whole is the ruthless suppression of the resistance of the exploiters, the organization of socialist construction, the mass training of men and women in the spirit of socialism and the gradual disappearance of classes." "The conquest of power by the proletariat is the violent overthrow of bourgeois power, the destruction of the capitalist state apparatus (bourgeois armies, police, bureaucratic hierarchy, the judiciary, parliaments, etc.) and substituting in its place new organs of proletarian power, to serve primarily as instruments for the suppression of the exploiters."[10]

DIALECTICAL METHOD

DIALECTICAL METHOD AND HEGEL'S THEOLOGY OF HISTORY

The intellectual basis of Marx's doctrine of the state is, as already pointed out, Hegel's philosophy of history, characterized by its dialectic method. The basic idea of this philosophy of history is that Reason governs the world and, consequently, world history.[11] This "Reason" implies morality whose laws "are the essential Rational."[12] The same idea is expressed by the statement that the history of the world is the "rational necessary course of the World-Spirit."[13] The World-Spirit is but the personification of Reason. This personification is essential. For the history of the world is also the realization of the will of the World-Spirit. The actions of the individuals and states of which history consists, are "the instruments and means of the World-Spirit for attaining its object";[14] and all historical men, in pursuing their own particular aims, execute only, without knowing it, "the will of the World-Spirit."[15] It is hardly possible to distinguish the will of the World-Spirit from the will of God. Hegel emphasizes that the idea: Reason directs the world, is an application of the "religious truth" that the world is not abandoned to chance but controlled by "Divine Providence," the "Providence of God." This Providence is "Wisdom endowed with an infinite Power which realizes its aim, viz. the absolute rational design of the world."[16] In investi-

---

[10] *Ibid.*
[11] G. W. F. Hegel, *Lectures on the Philosophy of History*, trans. from the first German ed. by J. Sibree (London, 1890), pp. 9, 12.
[12] *Ibid.*, p. 40.
[13] *Ibid.*, p. 11.
[14] *Ibid.*, p. 26.
[15] *Ibid.*, p. 31.
[16] *Ibid.*, p. 13.

gating the course of the World-Spirit in history, Hegel's philosophy constitutes the deliberate attempt of "knowing God" and expressly presents itself as such." Highly significant is the motto of his work: "The history of the world is not intelligible apart from a Government of the World." Hegel's so-called philosophy of history is the myth of the World-Spirit; it is not a philosophy, it is a *theology* of history. This fact cannot be without influence on the character of the philosophical and political systems based on this theology of history.

It is an essential element of a theological interpretation of the phenomena to assume that God is not only transcendent to, but at the same time, also immanent in the world, which is the manifestation of His will. Since His will is good, is the absolute value, reality must be considered to be perfect. The dualism of reality and value, the distinction between statements about reality and judgments of value—so characteristic of rationalistic science, cannot be recognized by theology, which is compelled to assume that value is inherent in reality and thus to identify the "is" with the "ought."

This view is the core of Hegel's philosophy, according to which world history is the realization of Reason representing the absolute logical as well as ethical value. If this assumption is true, then every historical event must be considered the work of the World-Spirit and as such reasonable and good. Indeed, Hegel terminates his work in affirming as its result "that what has happened, and is happening every day, is not only not without God, but is essentially His Work."[18] This is but another, and more sincere formulation of his most quoted thesis: The Real is the Rational and the Rational is the Real. If God is immanent in the world, if the absolute value is inherent in reality, there is no possibility of judging one actual event or one phase of history as better or worse than another; and if everything by its very nature is necessarily good, value judgments have lost any meaning. However, to distinguish between good and evil is the main task of theology in its capacity as ethics; and it is the specific function of a philosophy of history to differentiate by value judgments one historical event or one phase of history from the other. Without such differentiation a philosophy of history is meaningless. Theology satisfies its need

[17] *Ibid.*, p. 15.
[18] *Ibid.*, p. 477.

for distinguishing good and evil by introducing—at the cost of consistency—the devil as a countergod into the ethical interpretation of the world. Hegel's philosophy of history accomplishes the same result by the assumption that reality as manifested in world history is, though not perfect, yet on its way to perfection. World history is the progressive realization of Reason. This progress, which is the course of the World-Spirit, is a necessary one; for Reason as the "Sovereign" of the world is endowed with "infinite power."[19]

Since Hegel presents God as Reason, and everyone may understand by Reason what he thinks good and desirable, his theology of history is more flexible than the official Christian theology. Its thoroughly optimistic character, its thesis that the progressive realization of an ideal status of mankind is the necessary result of the historical process, must be welcome to the wishful thinking of any political ideology.

The conflict between the position that God is immanent in the world and, hence, value inherent in reality, on the one hand, and the necessity to differentiate in reality good and evil, on the other, presents itself in theology as the problem of theodicy. It is the problem how God, the omnipotent and absolutely good creator of the world, can ordain or permit the evil in nature and society. It is the central problem of theology. Hegel's philosophy proves to be a true theology of history by pretending to offer a solution of this problem. He states: "Our mode of treating the subject [the history of the world] is, in this aspect, a Theodicaea—a justification of the ways of God."[20] And at the end of his work, where he formulates the result of his philosophy in the above-quoted statement that all happenings are the work of God, Hegel says of his main thesis that the history of the world is the realization of the World-Spirit: "this is the true Theodicaea, the Justification of God in History."[21]

The essence of the problem of theodicy is the logical contradiction between two propositions, equally important to theology. The one is that God's will is absolute good; the other is that God's will is omnipotent, that nothing can happen without God's will and that, consequently, if there is evil in the world it must be there

---

[19] *Ibid.*, pp. 9, 11, 13.
[20] *Ibid.*, p. 16.
[21] *Ibid.*, p. 477.

by the will of God. As long as the logical law excluding contradiction, fundamental to rationalistic science, is considered to be valid, one of the two propositions cannot be true.

In order to reconcile his religious metaphysics, especially his theology of history with rationalistic science, the right of existence of which he does not deny but to which he assigns in his philosophical system only a subordinate position as compared with that of theology, Hegel has to invent a new logic. It is the synthetic logic of dialectic in contradistinction to the old analytical logic. The most characteristic element of the new logic of dialectic is the elimination of the law of contradiction, according to which two contradictory propositions cannot be true at the same time. Hegel tries to make us believe that in excluding contradiction the old logic commits a fundamental error. Contradiction is not only not a defect of thought, "speculative thought consists only in this that thought holds fast Contradiction and in Contradiction itself."[22] "In itself it is not, so to speak, a blemish, deficiency, or fault in a thing if a contradiction can be shown in it. On the contrary, every determination, every concrete, every concept is a union of ... moments which pass over ... into contradictory moments ... Finite things ... are contradictory in themselves."[23] In interpreting the relationship of two forces operating in opposite directions as "contradiction," Hegel projects the contradiction from thinking into being. Just as in nature and society two forces determining movements of opposite direction exist at the same time and result in a third movement in a new direction, so two contradictory propositions in thinking do not exclude each other but, as thesis and antithesis, produce, on a higher level, the synthesis: the unity in which the contradiction is resolved, and that means both overcome and preserved. It is contradiction that puts in motion things as well as thoughts. "Motion is existent contradiction in itself."[24] Contradiction is the principle of self-movement. It is a law of thought and at the same time a law of events.

The assumption that a law of thought can, at the same time, be a law of events, is based, in the last analysis, on the presupposition that the ethical as well as the logical value is inherent in reality,

---

[22] *Idem, Science of Logic,* trans. by W. H. Johnston and L. G. Struthers (London, 1929), II, p. 68.
[23] *Ibid.,* p. 70.
[24] *Ibid.,* p. 67.

that the Spirit is working in the historical events; that the Real is the Rational. This metaphysical hypothesis is at the basis of the fundamental fallacy in Hegel's dialectic: the identification of the relationship of opposite forces in external reality with the relationship of contradictory propositions in thinking. The relationship of two opposite forces resulting in a definite movement in nature and society has nothing to do with a logical contradiction. The phenomena concerned can, and must, be described by noncontradictory statements in complete conformity with the principles of the old logic. But it is precisely this fallacy of Hegel's dialectic that Marx has adopted for his dialectic. It is true that Marx declares: "My dialectic method is not only different from the Hegelian, but is its direct opposite. To Hegel, the life-process of the human brain, i.e. the process of thinking, which, under the name of 'the Idea,' he even transforms into an independent subject, is the demiurgos of the real world, and the real world is only the external, phenomenal form of 'the Idea.' With me, on the contrary, the idea is nothing else than the material world reflected by the human mind, and translated into forms of thought... With him [Hegel] it [dialectics] is standing on its head. It must be turned right side up again, if you would discover the rational kernel within the mystical shell."[25] Hegel is an idealist, Marx a materialist. But Marx, just as Hegel, understands by dialectic: evolution by means of contradiction, a contradiction of which Marx, just as Hegel, maintains that it is inherent in the social reality. The assumption of a "contradictory character" of evolution and especially of capitalistic society is an essential element of the historic or dialectic materialism founded by Marx.[26] Marx, just as Hegel, interprets conflicts in the struggle of life, the antagonism between groups of opposite interests, and especially the incongruity of productive forces and mode of production as logical con-

---

[25] Karl Marx, *Capital* (New York, 1906), p. 25.

[26] Cf. Engels, *Anti-Dühring*, pp. 131 ff., *passim;* Nikolai Bukharin, *Historical Materialism* (New York, 1928), pp. 72 ff. The basic fallacy of Hegel's dialectic: the interpretation of the antagonism of opposite forces as logical contradiction and the attempt to eliminate the logical law of contradiction, has been stigmatized as the "apex of absurdity" by Eugen Dühring in his *Cursus der Philosophie* (1875) and his *Kritische Geschichte der National-ökonomie und des Sozialismus* (1887). In the last-mentioned work, Dühring severely criticized Marx's social theory. It was against this work that Engels published his *Anti-Dühring* the main purpose of which was to defend Hegel's dialectic as adopted by Marx.

tradictions. Marx, just as Hegel, considers value as inherent in reality; but in contradistinction to Hegel and less consistent than the latter, he does not identify thinking and being. According to Marx, dialectic as a method of thinking "reflects" only the dialectic process in reality. The dialectic method must be used in order to grasp the dialectic of society. But in rejecting Hegel's identification of thinking and being, Marx deprives himself of the only possibility of justifying—at least to a certain extent—the fallacy of identifying the relationship of opposite forces in nature and society with logical contradiction.

Nothing can show more clearly the futility of the dialectic method than the fact that it enables Hegel to praise the state as a god, and Marx to curse it as a devil; that in applying this method the one affirms that the progressive realization of reason, by means of war, necessarily leads to the world domination of the German nation, whereas the other predicts, as the inevitable result of the historic evolution, the establishment, by means of revolution, of the free society of world communism. Such contradictory interpretations are possible because this philosophy, ignoring the unsurmountable dualism of reality and value, of the "is" and the "ought," presents what is merely a political postulate based on subjective value judgment, as the necessary result of evolution determined by objective laws and necessarily leading from a lower to a higher level of culture. If the actual reality does not correspond to the postulated value, allegedly inherent in it, the inexorable realization of this value is transferred to the future. Any historical situation may be interpreted to represent the thesis, or the antithesis, or the synthesis, according to its political evaluation by the interpreter. Thus, the dialectic method may be satisfactory to any political creed.

INTERPRETATION OF THE DIALECTICAL METHOD BY STALIN

The fact that the dialectical method may be used for any political purpose explains its extraordinary attractiveness, its world-wide spread, comparable only to the success of the natural-law doctrine in the eighteenth century. Just as the latter pretended to deduce from nature the principles of justice, the dialectic method pretends to deduce from history the correct political action. Hegel arrived at the conservative conclusion that unconditional submission to the authority of the established state is everyone's duty. He condemned Rousseau's doctrine that the authority of the state is based on a contract, and that means, on the consent of the individuals; for it led to revolution, and that means to "destroy the absolutely divine and its absolute authority and majesty."[27] The Marxists believe: History requires us to make revolution in order to destroy the state.

Nothing is more characteristic than the following passages in Joseph Stalin's essay *Dialectical and Historical Materialism.*[28]

... dialectics does not regard the process of development as a simple process of growth, where quantitative changes do not lead to qualitative changes, but as a development which passes from insignificant and imperceptible quantitative changes to open, fundamental changes, to qualitative changes; a development in which the qualitative changes occur not gradually, but rapidly and abruptly, taking the form of a leap from one state to another; they occur not accidentally but as the natural result of an accumulation of imperceptible and gradual quantitative changes.

The dialectical method therefore holds that the process of development should be understood not as a movement in a circle, not as a simple repetition of what has already occurred, but as an onward and upward movement, as a transition from an old qualitative state to a new qualitative state, as a development from the simple to the complex, from the lower to the higher.... dialectics holds that internal contradictions are inherent in all things and phenomena of nature, for they all have their negative and positive sides, a past and a future, something dying away and something developing; and that the struggle between these opposites, the struggle between the old and the new, between that which is dying away and that which is being born, between that which is disappearing and that which is developing, constitutes the internal content of the process of development, the internal content of the transformation of quantitative into qualitative changes.

The dialectical method therefore holds that the process of development from the lower to the higher takes place not as a harmonious unfolding of phenomena, but as a disclosure of the contradictions inherent in things and phenomena, as a "struggle" of opposite tendencies which operate on the basis of these contradictions.[29]

From these laws of development Stalin deduces the following practical consequences:

... if the passing of slow quantitative changes into rapid and abrupt qualitative changes is a law of development, then it is clear that revolutions made by oppressed classes are a quite natural and inevitable phenomenon.

---

[27] Hegel, *Philosophy of Right*, §258.
[28] Joseph Stalin, *Dialectical and Historical Materialism.* Little Lenin Library, vol. 25 (New York, 1940).
[29] *Ibid.*, pp. 8 f.

Hence the transition from capitalism to socialism and the liberation of the working class from the yoke of capitalism cannot be effected by slow changes, by reforms, but only by a qualitative change of the capitalist system, by revolution.

Hence, in order not to err in policy, one must be a revolutionary, not a reformist.

Further, if development proceeds by way of the disclosure of internal contradictions, by way of collisions between opposite forces on the basis of these contradictions and so as to overcome these contradictions, then it is clear that the class struggle of the proletariat is a quite natural and inevitable phenomenon.

Hence we must not cover up the contradictions of the capitalist system, but disclose and unravel them; we must not try to check the class struggle but carry it to its conclusion.

Hence, in order not to err in policy, one must pursue an uncompromising proletarian class policy, not a reformist policy of harmony of the interests of the proletariat and the bourgeoisie, not a compromisers' policy of "the growing of capitalism into socialism."

Such is the Marxist dialectical method when applied to social life, to the history of society.[30]

CONTRADICTIONS IN THE BOLSHEVIK DOCTRINE OF THE STATE

EVOLUTIONISM AND REVOLUTIONISM

"In order not to err in policy," one ought to be a revolutionary, uncompromising Bolshevik. In spite of the fact that communism, as interpreted by the Bolshevik doctrine, is the necessary and inevitable result of the law of evolution, revolution is postulated, and error, that is to say, a reformatory, non-Bolshevik attitude, is not excluded. Otherwise the terroristic suppression of all such "errors" was not necessary. This is evidently a contradiction. And this contradiction is the consequence of the syncretism of science and politics, inherent in the dialectical method. Dialectical materialism is an intellectual system which proudly presents itself as a science, able to predict future events determined by strict laws, as the "scientific" socialism, although it is merely a political doctrine in the specific sense of a political ideology used as an instrument in the struggle for power.

The contradictions resulting from the confusion of a scientific explanation of social reality and a political program are not the only ones that can be found in the Marxian doctrine of the state. Proponents of this doctrine are not at all disturbed by the fact

---

[30] *Ibid.*, pp. 14 f.

that it embodies basic contradictions. It is just the function of its dialectic to make a virtue of this necessity. A logic that eliminates the law of contradiction corresponds perfectly to the needs of an ideology the main purpose of which is not to explain in an objective-rational way the social phenomenon, but rather to justify or to reject, on the basis of subjective-emotional value judgments, a given social order. For such an ideology is by its very nature insensitive to, and consequently almost always entangled in, logical contradictions.

PURPOSE OF STATE: MAINTENANCE OR SUPPRESSION OF EXPLOITATION?

Another contradiction inherent in the Marxian doctrine lies in its definition of the state and the application of this definition to the dictatorship of the proletariat. The definition of the state is the typical example of the problematic influence value judgments may have on the allegedly scientific determination of a concept. According to the Marxian theory, the very essence of the state is its coercive machinery for the exploitation of one class by another, its function as the specific political instrument of capitalism. Only because the state is responsible for "capitalist slavery," "the untold horrors, savagery, absurdities and infamies of capitalist exploitation,"[31] to use Lenin's words, the destruction of this state by the socialist revolution is justified, and its replacement by a stateless society has to be considered as progress. The main objection that the Marxian doctrine puts forward against the "bourgeois" theory of the state is that the latter ignores the specific function of the coercive machinery called the state; and its specific function: to make the exploitation of the proletariat by the capitalists possible. But the dictatorship of the proletariat, established after the destruction of the bourgeois state, is still a true state, the "proletarian" state, and its essence is exactly the opposite of that of the bourgeois state: the definitive abolishment of all exploitation of one class by another. Both the bourgeois state and the proletarian state are centralized coercive orders, or, to use the Marxian terminology, both are coercive machineries. This is exactly the definition of the state which the Marxists try to ridicule as "formalistic" because it does not include the substantial purpose of this coercive

---

[31] Lenin, *State and Revolution*, pp. 73 f.

machinery, the content of this coercive order. But by its own use of the concept of state, Marxian doctrine shows that the coercive order we call the state may serve very different, even opposite purposes. If so, the purpose must not be included in a scientific definition of this phenomenon unless, in describing the dictatorship of the proletariat, two contradictory statements are to be maintained, that it is a state, and that it is not a state. Relying on Hegel's new logic, a Marxist may say that such contradiction shows only the dialectic character of the phenomena concerned. But how embarrassing it is to admit that the dictatorship of the proletariat is a state, although it should not be a state, manifests itself in the fact, that Lenin occasionally speaks of it as a "semi-state."[32] But, as a rule, he characterizes the dictatorship of the proletariat as the "proletarian state," and the official Bolshevik doctrine has never denied that the Soviet Union, the first successful dictatorship of the proletariat, is a "state." The "Program of the Communist International" expressly states that "the most suitable form of proletarian state is the Soviet State, a new type of state, which differs in principle from the bourgeois state not only in its class content but also in its internal structure."[33]

THE PROLETARIAN STATE
ACCORDING TO ENGELS

The contradiction which exists between the basic statement of the Marxian doctrine that the state by its very nature is a coercive machinery for the exploitation of the proletariat by the bourgeoisie, and the admission that there exists such a thing as the proletarian state, could be ignored by Engels—who developed this doctrine—since he considered the dictatorship of the proletariat a transitional stage of short duration. This notion clearly derives from the passage quoted above wherein he describes the establishment of the proletarian state as an act which automatically implies its self-abolition. As soon as the means of production are nationalized, and thus all class differences put to an end,—an achievement which may be accomplished in a relatively short time—the coercive machinery of the proletarian state, and that means the state itself, loses any justification and, according to Engels' prognosis, dis-

[32] *Ibid.*, p. 17.
[33] Program of the Communist International, *loc. cit.*, p. 187.

appears. That the men who actually control the coercive machinery and are in a position to use it for other purposes than to establish socialism, will voluntarily give up the power they possess, is the great miracle of the Marxian belief.

ACCORDING TO STALIN

At any rate, the first proletarian state, the Soviet Union, does not conform to Engels' prognosis. According to the most competent authority, it has achieved the purpose for which its coercive machinery has been put into motion: the establishment of socialism. In his report on the draft constitution of the U.S.S.R., Stalin characterized the situation in 1936 as follows:

But the most important thing is that capitalism has been banished entirely from the sphere of our industry, while the socialist form of production is now the system which has undivided sway in the sphere of our industry.... In the sphere of agriculture, instead of the ocean of small individual peasant farms with their poor technical equipment and strong kulak influence, we now have mechanized production, conducted on a scale larger than anywhere else in the world, with up-to-date technical equipment, in the form of an all-embracing system of collective farms and state farms.... Thus the complete victory of the socialist system in all spheres of national economy is now a fact. And what does this mean? It means that the exploitation of men by men has been abolished, eliminated, while the socialist ownership of the implements and means of production has been established as the unshakable foundation of our Soviet society. As a result of these changes in the sphere of the national economy of the U.S.S.R., we now have a new, socialist economy, which knows neither crises nor unemployment, which knows neither poverty nor ruin, and which provides citizens with every opportunity to lead a prosperous and cultured life.... In conformity with these changes in the sphere of the economy of the U.S.S.R., the *class structure* of our society has changed also.... all the exploiting classes have now been eliminated.... The proletariat is a class exploited by the capitalists. But, in our country, as you know, the capitalist class has already been eliminated, and the instruments and means of production have been taken from the capitalists and transferred to the state, of which the leading force is the working class. Consequently, there is no longer a capitalist class which could exploit the working class. Consequently, our working class, far from being bereft of the instruments and means of production, on the contrary, possess them jointly with the whole people. And since it possesses them, and the capitalist class has been eliminated, all possibility of the working class being exploited is precluded.... can our working class be called the proletariat? Clearly, it cannot.... the proletariat of the U.S.S.R. has been transformed into an entirely new class, into the working class of the U.S.S.R. which has abolished the capitalist economic system, which has established the socialist ownership of the instruments and means of production and is directing Soviet society along the road to communism. [And, finally he summarizes:] Our Soviet society has already, in the main, succeeded in achieving socialism; it has created a socialist system, *i.e.*, it has brought about what Marxists in other words call the first, or lower, phase of communism. Hence, in the main, we have already achieved the first phase of communism, socialism.[34]

The "Withering Away" of the State
ACCORDING TO ENGELS

The achievement of socialism is, according to Engels, the moment when the proletarian state disappears. In transforming the means of production into state property, the proletariat, he says, "puts an end to itself as the proletariat, it puts an end to class differences and class antagonisms, it puts an end also to the state as state." "The first act in which the state really comes forward as the representation of society as a whole—the seizure of the means of production in the name of society—is, at the same time, its last independent act as a state."[35] When, as Stalin testifies, "the instruments and means of production have been taken from the capitalists and transferred to the state," when "all the exploiting classes have been eliminated," when "the proletariat has been transformed into the working class" of a socialist society, the coercive machinery of the state must automatically wither away.

ACCORDING TO STALIN

There can be no doubt that Soviet Russia, although it has ceased to be a dictatorship of the proletariat, has not ceased to be a dictatorship, and there are not the slightest symptoms of this state's withering away. The nationalization of the means of production is certainly not the "last independent act" of the state "as a state." According to Stalin, Soviet society is free from exploitation, it is a classless society in the sense that there exist no class antagonisms. But Soviet society has not yet reached the higher phase of communism in which the ruling principle will be the formula: from each according to his ability, to each according to his needs. The principle of the actual phase of Russian communism is still: from each according to his ability, to each according to his work. But the progress from the latter to the former is—according to the original doctrine as presented by Engels—not a function of the

---

[34] Stalin, *Leninism, Selected Writings* (New York, 1942), pp. 381–386.
[35] Cf. above, p. 12.

coercive machinery of the state as such. Lenin, in his *State and Revolution,* it is true, declares: "The state will be able to wither away completely when society has realized the rule: From each according to his ability, to each according to his needs."[36] This statement may, or may not, be correct, but it is certainly not based on Engels' theory of the state's withering away. According to this theory, the coercive machinery of the proletarian state is necessary only to suppress exploitation and class antagonisms, but not to increase the production of socialist economy to the highest possible degree. Since socialist economy will best prosper in a stateless society, it is difficult to understand why it is necessary to maintain the coercive machinery of the state after "the complete victory of the socialist system in all spheres of the national economy." Since there is no longer any class to suppress, since there are no longer any class differences and class antagonisms within Soviet society, there is no reason for the continued existence of the coercive machinery of the state.

CAPITALIST ENCIRCLEMENT

If the internal situation in 1936 has been correctly described by Stalin, there is no room for a government, and certainly no room for the secret police in Soviet Russia. But neither the one nor the other show any intention of disappearing. And this is quite understandable. For, the coercive machinery is necessary not only, as Engels taught, to nationalize the means of production, to liquidate the class of exploiters, to abolish all class differences and class antagonisms, to establish a socialist society, but also to maintain it and to defend it against disturbances from the inside and attacks from the outside. The doctrine that the state will wither away when socialism is established, is based on the utopian assumption that in a socialist society there will be no reasons for violating the social order, since this order will guarantee to everyone the highest possible degree of happiness. In his report on the constitution, Stalin declared that after socialism has been established "a constitution"—and that means a coercive state machinery—"is needed for the purpose of consolidating a social order desired by and beneficial to the toilers." If such "consolidating," and hence a "state," is still necessary after socialism "has been established as

---

[36] Lenin, *op. cit.,* p. 79.

the unshakable foundation of Soviet society," then there is no phase of communism where a "state" will be superfluous and "wither away." In an interview with foreign workers delegations, which asked why the G.P.U. has not yet been dissolved, Stalin said:

From the point of view of the internal situation, the revolution is so firm and unshakable that we could do without the G.P.U. But the trouble is that the enemies at home are not isolated individuals. They are connected in a thousand ways with the capitalists of all countries who support them by every means and in every way. We are a country surrounded by capitalist states. The internal enemies of our revolution are the agents of the capitalists of all countries. The capitalist states are the background and basis for the internal enemies of our revolution. In fighting against the enemies at home we fight the counter-revolutionary elements of all countries. Judge for yourselves whether under such conditions we can do without such punitive organs as the G.P.U.[37]

In his "Report to the Eighteenth Congress of the Communist Party of the Soviet Union," delivered March 10, 1939,[38] Stalin directly and extensively dealt with the problem of the state's "withering away." Since his statements represent the official doctrine of Bolshevism on the most important point of the Marxian theory of the state, they are here quoted as completely as necessary. They appear in Section 4 of the Report under the heading "Some Questions of Theory." Stalin says: "Another of the defects of our propagandist and ideological work is the absence of full clarity among our comrades on certain theoretical questions of vital practical importance, the existence of a certain amount of confusion on these questions. I refer to the question of the state in general, and of our Socialist state in particular, and to the question of our Soviet intelligentsia." It is highly significant that the "questions of theory" are dealt with from the angle of the "propagandist and ideological work" of the Communist party. That "theory" in general, and the theory of the state in particular, is to be used as an instrument of politics is taken for granted. "It is sometimes asked," says Stalin, " 'We have abolished the exploiting classes; there are no longer any hostile classes in the country; there is nobody to suppress; hence there is no more need for the state; it must die away. Why then do we not help our Socialist state to die away? Why do we not strive to put an end to it? Is it not time

---

[37] The interview took place on November 5, 1927; cf. Stalin, *Leninism*, Vol. II (New York, 1933), p. 99.
[38] Stalin, *Leninism* (London, 1942), pp. 656–665.

to throw out all this rubbish of a state?' Or further: 'The exploiting classes have already been abolished in our country; Socialism has been built in the main; we are advancing towards Communism. Now, the Marxist doctrine of the state says that there is to be no state under Communism. Why then do we not help our Socialist state to die away? Is it not time we relegated the state to the museum of antiquities?' " Such questions are quite natural; for they result from all that Marx and Engels taught about the nature of the state. But according to Stalin, to ask such questions proves complete misunderstanding of the Marxian theory of the state.

These questions show that those who ask them have conscientiously memorized certain propositions contained in the doctrine of Marx and Engels about the state. But they also show that these comrades have failed to understand the essential meaning of this doctrine; that they have failed to realize in what historical conditions the various propositions of this doctrine were elaborated; and, what is more, that they do not understand present-day international conditions, have overlooked the capitalist encirclement and the dangers it entails for the Socialist country. These questions not only betray an underestimation of the capitalist encirclement but also an underestimation of the role and significance of the bourgeois states and their organs, which send spies, assassins and wreckers into our country and are waiting for a favourable opportunity to attack it by armed force. They likewise betray an underestimation of the role and significance of our Socialist state and of its military, punitive and intelligence organs, which are essential for the defence of the Socialist land from foreign attack. It must be confessed that the comrades mentioned are not the only ones to sin in this underestimation. All the Bolsheviks, all of us without exception, sin to a certain extent in this respect. Is it not surprising that we learned about the espionage and conspiratorial activities of the Trotskyite and Bukharinite leaders only quite recently, in 1937 and 1938, although, as the evidence shows, these gentry were in the services of foreign espionage organizations and carried on conspiratorial activities from the very first days of the October Revolution? How could we have failed to notice so grave a matter? How are we to explain this blunder? The usual answer to this question is that we could not possibly have assumed that these people could have fallen so low. But that is no explanation, still less is it a justification; for the blunder was a blunder. How is this blunder to be explained? It is to be explained by an underestimation of the strength and consequence of the mechanism of the bourgeois states surrounding us and of their espionage organs, which endeavour to take advantage of people's weaknesses, their vanity, their slackness of will, to enmesh them in their espionage nets and use them to surround the organs of the Soviet state. It is to be explained by an underestimation of the role and significance of the mechanism of our Socialist state and of its intelligence service, by an underestimation of this intelligence service, by the twaddle that an intelligence service in a Soviet state is an unimportant trifle, and that the Soviet intelligence service and the Soviet state itself will soon have to be relegated to the museum of antiquities.[39]

Even after the establishment of socialism in the Soviet Union, the coercive machinery of the state cannot be allowed to wither away because of the international situation, the "capitalist encirclement." To avoid the admission that the coercive machinery is also necessary because of the internal situation—because it is necessary to suppress the opposition within the Bolshevik party, the movement led by Trotsky and Bukharin is presented as activity "in the service of foreign espionage organizations." The possibility that there could be an opposition to the policy of the Bolshevik party in no connection with hostile capitalist states, an opposition which wished to establish and to maintain true socialism in a different way from that of the Bolshevik party, is out of the question, according to Stalin.

DECISIVE MODIFICATION OF THE MARX-ENGELS DOCTRINE

It is evident that Engels in propounding the doctrine of the state's withering away did not take into consideration the international situation of a state which is the only one that has established socialism. With reference to this fact Stalin maintains "that certain of the general propositions in the Marxist doctrine of the state were incompletely worked out and inadequate. It received currency owing to our unpardonably heedless attitude to matters pertaining to the theory of the state, in spite of the fact that we have twenty years of practical experience in matters of state which provide rich material for theoretical generalizations, and in spite of the fact that, given the desire, we have every opportunity of successfully filling this gap in theory." It is especially Engels' proposition that the state will "wither away," which needs further development. "Is this proposition of Engels' correct?" asks Stalin. This is his answer:

Yes, it is correct, but only on one of two conditions: (1) *if* we study the Socialist state only from the angle of the internal development of the country, abstracting ourselves in advance from the international factor, isolating, for the convenience of investigation, the country and the state from the international situation; or (2) *if* we assume that Socialism is already victorious in

---

[39] *Ibid.*, pp. 656 f.

all countries, or in the majority of countries, that a Socialist encirclement exists instead of a capitalist encirclement, that there is no more danger of foreign attack, and that there is no more need to strengthen the army and the state.

Well, but what if Socialism has been victorious only in one country, taken singly, and if in view of this, it is quite impossible to abstract oneself from international conditions—what then? Engels' formula does not furnish an answer to this question. As a matter of fact, Engels did not set himself this question, and therefore could not have given an answer to it. Engels proceeds from the assumption that Socialism has already been victorious in all countries or in a majority of countries, more or less simultaneously. Consequently Engels is not here investigating any specific Socialist state of any particular country, but the development of the Socialist state in general, on the assumption that Socialism has been victorious in a majority of countries—according to the formula: "assuming that Socialism is victorious in a majority of countries, what changes must the proletarian, Socialist state undergo?" Only this general and abstract character of the problem can explain why in his investigation of the question of the Socialist state Engels completely abstracted himself from such a factor as international conditions, the international situation.

But it follows from this that Engels' general formula about the destiny of the Socialist state in general cannot be extended to the partial and specific case of the victory of Socialism in one country only, a country which is surrounded by a capitalist world, is subject to the menace of foreign military attack, cannot therefore abstract itself from the international situation, and must have at its disposal a well-trained army, well-organized punitive organs, and a strong intelligence service—consequently must have its own state, strong enough to defend the conquests of Socialism from foreign attack.[40]

The "gap" in the Marxian theory of the state: that the founders of scientific socialism ignored the necessity of maintaining the coercive machinery of the state even after the establishment of socialism, if such achievement is reached only within one state, has not been filled by Lenin. He, too, did not interpret the dogma of the state's withering away to mean that it does not apply to an isolated socialist state. Consequently, Stalin must not only correct Marx and Engels, but also—and this is a rather delicate task for a Bolshevik—Lenin. He says:

Lenin wrote his famous book, *The State and Revolution*, in August 1917, that is, a few months before the October Revolution and the establishment of the Soviet state. Lenin considered it the main task of this book to defend Marx's and Engels' doctrine of the state from the distortions and vulgarizations of the opportunists. Lenin was preparing to write a second volume of *The State*

---

[40] *Ibid.*, pp. 658 f.

and Revolution, in which he intended to sum up the principal lessons of the experience of the Russian revolutions of 1905 and 1917. There can be no doubt that Lenin intended in the second volume of his book to elaborate and develop the theory of the state on the basis of the experience gained during the existence of Soviet power in our country. Death, however, prevented him from carrying this task into execution. But what Lenin did not manage to do should be done by his disciples.[41]

Under the protection of Lenin's ghost Stalin presents the new, the improved Marxian doctrine of the state:

The state arose because society split up into antagonistic classes; it arose in order to keep in restraint the exploited majority in the interests of the exploiting minority. The instruments of state authority have been mainly concentrated in the army, the punitive organs, the espionage service, the prisons. Two basic functions characterize the activity of the state: at home (the main function), to keep in restraint the exploited majority; abroad (not the main function), to extend the territory of its class, the ruling class, at the expense of the territory of other states, or to defend the territory of its own state from attack by other states. Such was the case in slave society and under feudalism. Such is the case under capitalism.

In order to overthrow capitalism it was not only necessary to remove the bourgeoisie from power, it was not only necessary to expropriate the capitalists, but also to smash entirely the bourgeois state machine and its old army, its bureaucratic officialdom and its police force and to substitute for it a new, proletarian form of state, a new, Socialist state. And that, as we know, is exactly what the Bolsheviks did. But it does not follow that the new proletarian state may not preserve certain functions of the old state, changed to suit the requirements of the proletarian state. Still less does it follow that the forms of our Socialist state must remain unchanged, that all the original functions of our state must be fully preserved in future. As a matter of fact, the forms of our state are changing and will continue to change in line with the development of our country and with the changes in the international situation.[42]

So far, the new doctrine is identical with the old one. More interesting is the way Stalin characterizes the development of the Russian socialist state.

Since the October Revolution, our Socialist state has passed through two main phases in its development.

The first phase was the period from the October Revolution to the elimination of the exploiting classes. The principal task in that period was to suppress the resistance of the overthrown classes, to organize the defence of the country against the attack of the interventionists, to restore industry and agriculture,

---

[41] *Ibid.,* p. 660.
[42] *Ibid.,* pp. 661 f.

and to prepare the conditions for the elimination of the capitalist elements. Accordingly in this period our state performed two main functions. The first function was to suppress the overthrown classes inside the country. In this respect our state bore a superficial resemblance to previous states whose functions had also been to suppress recalcitrants, with the fundamental difference, however, that our state suppressed the exploiting minority in the interests of the labouring majority, while previous states had suppressed the exploited majority in the interests of the exploiting minority. The second function was to defend the country from foreign attack. In this respect it likewise bore a superficial resemblance to previous states, which also undertook the armed defence of their countries, with the fundamental difference, however, that our state defended from foreign attack the gains of the labouring majority, while previous states in such cases defended the wealth and privileges of the exploiting minority. Our state had yet a third function: this was the work of economic organization and cultural education performed by our state bodies with the purpose of developing the infant shoots of the new, Socialist economic system and re-educating the people in the spirit of Socialism. But this new function did not attain to any considerable development in that period.

The second phase was the period from the elimination of the capitalist elements in town and country to the complete victory of the Socialist economic system and the adoption of the new Constitution. The principal task in this period was to establish the Socialist economic system all over the country and to eliminate the last remnants of the capitalist elements, to bring about a cultural revolution, and to form a thoroughly modern army for the defence of the country. And the functions of our Socialist state changed accordingly. The function of military suppression inside the country ceased, died away; for exploitation has been abolished, there were no more exploiters left, and so there was no one to suppress. In place of this function of suppression the state acquired the function of protecting Socialist property from thieves and pilferers of the people's property. The function of defending the country from foreign attack fully remained; consequently the Red Army and the Navy also fully remained, as did the punitive organs and the intelligence service, which are indispensable for the detection and punishment of the spies, assassins and wreckers sent into our country by foreign espionage services. The function of economic organization and cultural education by the state organs also remained, and was developed to the full. Now the main task of our state inside the country is the work of peaceful economic organization and cultural education. As for our army, punitive organs, and intelligence service, their edge is no longer turned to the inside of the country but to the outside, against external enemies.[43]

The statement that "the function of military suppression inside the country ceased, died away," is rather problematic in view of the fact that "the Red Army and the Navy fully remained." And it is not very consistent to maintain that the "punitive organs and

---

[43] *Ibid.*, pp. 661 f.

the intelligence service" must remain only "for the detection and punishment of the spies, assassins and wreckers sent by foreign espionage services" when it is admitted that the state has still the "function of protecting socialist property from thieves and pilferers of the people's property," who are not sent by foreign espionage services and who may threaten the socialist economic system even after the "capitalist encirclement" will have disappeared. Is protection from such criminals possible without "punitive organs," and that means, a coercive machinery? But, in summarizing the results of the new theory of state, Stalin maintains the thesis that the coercive machinery of the state must be maintained only for defense against external aggression. He says: "Will our state remain in the period of Communism also?" And he answers: "Yes, it will, unless the capitalist encirclement is liquidated and unless the danger of foreign military attack has disappeared. Naturally, of course, the forms of our state will again change in conformity with the changes in the situation at home and abroad. No, it will not remain and will atrophy if the capitalist encirclement is liquidated and a Socialist encirclement takes its place."[44]

THE SOCIALIST WORLD STATE: THE LAST STATE

So long as the socialist state is surrounded by capitalist states, it will remain a true state. The last phase of communism: the stateless society, cannot be expected until world revolution has destroyed, at least, most of the capitalist states. But even if all the states of the world were socialist states, the "state" as an institution could hardly be allowed to wither away. For so long as there exists a plurality of national states rivalry among them and hence war is not excluded. If such violent antagonism within one and the same socialist party was possible—as actually took place within the Bolshevik party—why would war between socialist states be excluded, especially if socialism is organized in a different way in the different states? Only a socialist world state will make possible a disarmament, which those who believe in Engels' prophecy may interpret as the first step toward the state's withering away. This idea is exactly what the "Program of the Communist International" proclaims.

---

[44] *Ibid.*, p. 662.

The dictatorship of the world proletariat is an essential and vital condition precedent to the transition of world capitalist economy to socialist economy. This world dictatorship can be established only when the victory of Socialism has been achieved in certain countries or groups of countries, when the newly established proletarian republics enter into a federal union with the already existing proletarian republics, when the number of such federations has grown and extended also to the colonies which have emancipated themselves from the yoke of imperialism; when these federations of republics have finally grown into a world union of Soviet Socialist Republics uniting the whole of mankind under the hegemony of the international proletariat organized as a State.[45]

The Communist International formally dissolved itself in the spring of 1943. But what was true until this date, is still true today: that the coercive machinery of the socialist state cannot be disposed of so long as within most of the other states capitalism is still maintained, and that, consequently, it is the world state only which may wither away.[46] Thus the ultimate goal of communism seems to be transferred to so distant a future that it is hardly worth while to examine seriously the question whether a stateless society is really possible, and especially whether the replacement of the economic anarchy of the capitalist system by a strictly planned economy is compatible with the political anarchy of the last phase of communism.[47]

---

[45] Program of the Communist International, *loc. cit.*, p. 185.

[46] In his "Problems of Leninism" in *Leninism* (London, 1942, pp. 153 f.), Stalin examines the "question of the victory of socialism in one country." He says that this problem implies two different questions. First there is "the question of the possibility of building socialism by the efforts of one country, which must be answered in the affirmative." Then there is the question of "whether a country in which the dictatorship of the proletariat has been established can consider itself fully guaranteed against intervention, and consequently against the restoration of the old order, without a victorious revolution in a number of other countries, which must be answered in the negative." From these statements it follows that the "withering away" of the state can take place only after the victory of the socialist revolution—at least in a number of other countries.

[47] Neither Marx nor Engels has systematically discussed the problem how a society organized under a highly centralized economic system is possible without an order providing coercive acts as sanctions to be inflicted upon those who violate the order. Lenin, it is true, deals with this problem in his *State and Revolution*, but all he has to say, is this: "We are no utopians, and we do not in the least deny the possibility and inevitability of excesses on the part of individual persons, nor the need to suppress such excesses. But, in the first place, no special machinery, no special apparatus of repression is needed for this; this will be done by the armed people itself, as simply and as readily as any crowd of civilized people even in modern society, parts a pair of combatants or does not allow a woman to be outraged. And, secondly, we know that the fundamental social cause of excesses which consist in violating the rules of social life is the exploitation of the masses, their want and their

poverty. With the removal of this chief cause, excesses will inevitably begin to wither away. We do not know how quickly and in what succession, but we know that they will wither away. With their withering away, the state will also 'wither away.'" The state will wither away owing to the simple fact that "freed from capitalist slavery, from the untold horrors, savagery, absurdities and infamies of capitalist exploitation, people will gradually become accustomed to observance of the elementary rules of social life that have been known for centuries and repeated for thousands of years in all school books. They will become accustomed to observing them without force, without compulsion, without subordination, without a special apparatus for compulsion which is called the state" (pp. 73–75). What are "the elementary rules of social life that have been known for centuries" which Lenin has in mind? The principles of capitalist morality? And will the social order of a communist society with its highly complex plan of economic production and distribution really be so "elementary" that no legal apparatus will be necessary to guarantee the strictest obedience, on which the working of this plan depends? Is it possible to establish and maintain planned economy "without subordination" of those who are obliged to execute the plan to those who have the power to draft it, to enact it, and to make it obligatory? The decisive point is that the main causes of violations of the social order result from exploitation, and that, consequently, there will be no such violations in a socialist society; people will become accustomed to obey the rules of the social order without force. This is an unproved and unprovable statement.

Part Two

DEMOCRACY OR PARTY DICTATORSHIP

DEMOCRACY OR PARTY DICTATORSHIP

Marx's and Engels' Attitude Toward Democracy

THE WRITINGS of Marx and Engels give a relatively clear answer to the question of the form of government to be established in the proletarian state. The Communist Manifesto states: "The first step in the revolution by the working class is the raising of the proletariat to the position of ruling class and to establish democracy." And Engels writes in his "Kritik des sozial-demokratischen Programmentwurfes 1891 :"[1] "If anything is certain it is that our party and the working class can only come to power under the form of the democratic republic. This is, indeed, the specific form for the dictatorship of the proletariat, as has already been shown by the great French Revolution ..."

There is no reason to assume that the suggestion of Marx and Engels that the proletarian state be organized as a democracy must be interpreted to mean that the concept of democracy as established in the proletarian state is different from the concept of democracy as established in the capitalist state. The concept of democracy as used by Marx and Engels is the traditional concept according to which a state is a democracy if it fulfills certain requirements of political freedom in a positive as well as in a negative sense. Nothing in the writings of Marx and Engels supports the assumption that the democracy they expected to be established by the dictatorship of the proletariat would be compatible with the dictatorship of one political party, excluding all others, especially socialist parties fighting for the emancipation of the working class. In their doctrine of the dictatorship of the proletariat, Marx and Engels took it for granted that the proletariat, at the moment of the revolution, would form the overwhelming majority of the people and would be united by a class consciousness strong enough to make undisputed leadership by one socialist party possible. The only difference between the democracy of the capitalist state and the democracy of the proletarian state considered by Marx and Engels was that the constitution of the proletarian state would be more democratic than that of the capitalist state. The Paris Commune of 1871 was, in the eyes of Marx and Engels, a kind of experiment in proletarian revolution. What they approved

---

[1] *Neue Zeit*, XX–I, 1901/1902, p. 11.

of in this experiment was the fact that the Commune was formed by universal suffrage, that the officials were elective, responsible, and revocable.[2] These are typical elements of democracy as realized also in capitalist states.

DEMOCRACY AND REVOLUTION

PEACEFUL ESTABLISHMENT OF SOCIALISM

The recognition of democracy as the form of government of the proletarian state is not quite consistent with the doctrine that the only way to establish this state is by the revolutionary employment of force, which is certainly not a democratic method; and with the characterization of the proletarian state as "dictatorship," which is the contrary of democracy. If, in a democratic republic with a capitalist economy, the very political situation exists that enables the proletarian revolution to establish the proletarian state as a democracy—the proletariat forming the majority of the people and ready to replace capitalism by socialism—there is no reason to employ force. The nationalization of the means of production and all the other measures necessary to abolish exploitation, class differences, and class antagonisms may be accomplished by legislative and administrative acts in a peaceful and constitutional way. This is exactly what is now happening in England under the government of the Labour party. Even Marx occasionally admitted such a possibility. In 1871, at the time of the Commune, Marx wrote in a letter to Kugelmann, "that the next attempt of the French Revolution must be: not, as in the past, to transfer the bureaucratic and military machinery from one hand to the other, but to smash that machine; and this is the precondition of any real people's revolution on the Continent."[3] Here, Marx restricts the necessity of revolution to the European continent. He assumed that a peaceful victory of socialism was not excluded in Great Britain and the United States. In 1872, in an address delivered in a public meeting after the closure of the Hague Congress of the International, he said: "The worker must one day capture political power in order to found the new organization of labor. He must reverse the old policy which the old constitutions maintain if he will not, like the Christians of old who

---

[2] Cf. Engels, Introduction to Marx, *The Civil War in France* (New York, 1940), p. 21.

[3] *Neue Zeit*, XX–I, 1901/1902, p. 709.

despised and neglected such things, renounce the things of this world. But we do not assert that the way to reach this goal is the same everywhere. We know that the institutions, manners and customs of the various countries must be considered, and we do not deny that there are countries, like England and America, and if I understood your arrangements better, I might even add Holland—where the worker may attain his object by peaceful means. But not in all countries is this the case."[4] Here, Marx admits that even on the Eureopean continent socialism may be established without revolution. Any interpretation of Marx which sincerely accepts his doctrine that the proletarian state shall have the character of a democracy, must take these statements very seriously.

REVOLUTIONARY ESTABLISHMENT OF SOCIALISM

Lenin, who usually is inclined to believe in Marx as in an infallible authority, tries to prove that his master was wrong when he admitted the possibility of a peaceful development of the capitalist into the proletarian democracy. He says in his *State and Revolution:* "Today, in 1917, in the epoch of the first great imperialist war, this exception made by Marx (in the letter to Kugelmann) is no longer valid. Both England and America, the greatest and last representatives of Anglo-Saxon 'liberty' in the sense of the absence of militarism and bureaucracy, have today plunged headlong into the all-European dirty, bloody morass of military bureaucratic institutions to which everything is subordinated and which trample everything under foot. Today, both in England and in America, the 'precondition of any real people's revolution' is the smashing, the destruction of the 'ready-made state-machinery' (brought in those countries, between 1914 and 1917, to general 'European' imperialist perfection)."[5] The statement that in Great Britain and in the United States "military bureaucratic institutions" prevail "to which everything is subordinated and which trample everything under foot" was, even in 1917, during the

---

[4] Quoted by Karl Kautsky, *The Dictatorship of the Proletariat*, 2d ed. (Manchester, 1920), pp. 9 ff.

[5] V. I. Lenin, *State and Revolution*, p. 34. Stalin, in his "Foundations of Leninism" in *Leninism* (New York, 1928, I, pp. 115–117), unconditionally adheres to this opinion of Lenin's. He says that "Marx's reservation 'on the Continent' had become obsolete, and what he said of continental Europe applied with equal force to Britain and the United States." That Marx admitted the possibility of a peaceful development of bourgeois democracy into proletarian democracy also for the European continent, is ignored.

First World War, a gross exaggeration. If it is maintained as a description of the peacetime situation in the two countries, it is certainly without foundation. No democratic constitution can work in time of war without restrictions. In time of peace, however, there may be imperialism, militarism, and bureaucracy and, nevertheless, a democratic constitution may be in force which would make it possible for a socialist majority to bring into power, by peaceful means, a socialist government.

DEMOCRACY AND CAPITALISM

It may be that in a capitalist state with a thoroughly democratic constitution the proletariat does not form the majority of the people, or despite the fact that it forms the majority there is not a socialist majority; or there are two or more socialist parties opposed to one another. There can be little doubt that this is often so, and it is perhaps the explanation of the fact that true democracy is possible in a capitalist state. Under such political circumstances, it is an obvious fiction to speak of suppression of the majority, namely, the proletariat, by the minority, the bourgeoisie. Under such political circumstances, a revolutionary movement for the realization of socialism can lead only to a true dictatorship, the dictatorship of a minority over the majority, and especially to the dictatorship of one socialist party. It may be that in many countries and even in those which have a democratic constitution the political situation is of the kind just mentioned. Only then is revolution necessary to realize socialism; and then socialism is incompatible with democracy. It seems that these were the circumstances under which socialism was established in Soviet Russia.

ESTABLISHMENT OF SOCIALISM IN RUSSIA

After Russia had been proclaimed a republic on September 1, 1917, it was about to become a democracy. The Provisional Government which was overthrown by the Bolshevik Revolution was certainly not guilty of any attempt to suppress politically the proletariat; and the proletariat was certainly not the majority of the Russian people. This fact was admitted even by writers who belonged to the Bolshevik party. Thus, for instance, Radek declared immediately after the coming into power of the Bolshevik party: "In Russia the proletariat forms certainly only a minority of the population.''[6] This may explain why Lenin places such extraordinary stress on the thesis that the only way to establish the dictatorship of the proletariat is by "violent revolution." Stalin, who in this point follows Lenin, answers the question of whether the establishment of socialism is possible without "violent revolution," as follows: "Obviously not. To think that such a revolution can be carried out peacefully within the framework of bourgeois democracy, which is adapted to the domination of the bourgeoisie, means one of two things. It means either madness, and the loss of normal human understanding, or else an open and gross repudiation of the proletarian revolution."[7] To prove this point, he quotes Lenin:

Let the majority of the population, while private property is still maintained, that is while the power and oppression of capital are maintained, declare itself for the party of the proletariat. Only then can it, and should it, take power. That is what is said by petty-bourgeois democrats who call themselves "socialists" but are really the henchmen of the bourgeoisie. . . . But we say: Let the revolutionary proletariat first overthrow the bourgeoisie, break the yoke of capital and smash the bourgeois state machine; then the victorious proletariat will be able rapidly to gain the sympathy and support of the majority of the toiling non-proletarian masses by satisfying their needs at the expense of the exploiters.[8] . . . In order to win the majority of the population, the proletariat must, in the first place, overthrow the bourgeoisie and seize state power; secondly, it must set up a Soviet government and smash to pieces the old state machinery, whereby it immediately undermines the rule, authority and influence of the bourgeoisie and of the petty-bourgeois compromisers over the non-proletarian toiling masses; thirdly, it must entirely destroy the influence of the bourgeoisie and of the petty-bourgeois compromisers over the majority of the non-proletarian toiling masses by revolutionary satisfaction of their economic needs at the expenses of the exploiters.[9]

ABANDONMENT OF THE POSTULATE OF DEMOCRACY

The fact that in Russia the dictatorship of the proletariat could be established by a minority only, and that democracy in the ordinary sense of the term was hardly possible as the political form of this dictatorship, may also explain why Lenin's statements concerning democracy as the form of government of the proletarian state are so ambiguous and contradictory. Other theorists of Bol-

---

[6] Karl Radek, *The Development of Socialism from Science to Action.* German ed. (Vienna, 1918), p. 18.
[7] Stalin, *Leninism* (London, 1942), p. 126.
[8] Lenin, *Selected Works*, Russian ed. Vol. VI, pp. 482–483.
[9] *Ibid.*, p. 475.

shevism were more sincere in this respect and openly admitted
that the Revolution of 1917 did not and could not establish democracy. Bukharin, for instance, makes no attempt to present the
government established by the Bolshevik Revolution as democratic.
He contrasts the Soviet constitution with the "antiquated form
of a parliamentary bourgeois republic (sometimes called 'democratic')." But, in repudiating the "parliamentary bourgeois republic," he rejects the general idea of democracy. For he says:
"What is the essential difference between a parliamentary republic
and a republic of soviets? It is, that in a soviet republic the non-
working elements are deprived of the franchise and take no part
in administrating affairs. . . . The bourgeoisie, ex-landowners,
bankers, speculating traders, merchants, shopkeepers, usurers, the
Korniloff intellectuals, priests and bishops, in short the whole of
the black host have no right to vote, no fundamental political
rights."[10] This was exactly the difference between the Bolsheviki,
the left wing of the Russian socialist party, and the Mensheviki,
the right wing, that the latter were for democracy and the former
were not. In his famous pamphlet *From October to Brest-Litowsk*,
Leon Trotsky writes: "More than once, the Philistines called our
attention to the fact that the new dumas and zemstvos elected on
the basis of universal suffrage, were incomparably more democratic than the soviets and were more suited to represent the
population. However, this formal democratic criterion is devoid
of serious content in a revolutionary epoch."[11] "Formal" democracy is identical with democracy, since democracy is by its very
nature a form of government. Trotsky says: "As Marxists, we have
never been idol-worshippers of formal democracy." But, in the
following statement, he openly declares that democracy—and not
only "formal" democracy—is not an essential element of Marxian
socialism.

In a society of classes, democratic institutions not only do not eliminate class
struggle, but [they] also give to class interests an utterly imperfect expression. . . . And democratic institutions become a still less perfect medium for
the expression of the class struggle under revolutionary circumstances . . . The
ponderous machinery of democratic institutions lags behind this [revolu-
tionary] evolution all the more, the bigger the country and the less perfect its
technical apparatus.[12]

[10] N. Bukharin, *The Communist Program* (New York, 1920), pp. 23 ff.
[11] Leon Trotsky, *From October to Brest-Litowsk* (New York, 1919), p. 28.
[12] *Ibid.*

Against Kautsky he says:

He tries to prove that for the working class it is always expedient, in the long run, to preserve the essential elements of the democratic order. This is, of course, true as a general rule. But Kautsky has reduced this historical truth to professorial banality. If, in the final analysis, it is to the advantage of the proletariat to introduce its class struggle and even its dictatorship, through the channels of democratic institutions, it does not at all follow that history always affords it the opportunity of attaining this happy consumation. There is nothing in the Marxian theory to warrant the deduction that history always creates such conditions as are most "favorable" to the proletariat.[13]

Trotsky states that the "Right Social Revolutionists" received "a majority in the Constituent Assembly," "owing to the clumsy electoral democratic machinery." In applying the dialectic method, he interprets the situation as a "contradiction." "The result was a contradiction which was absolutely irreducible within the limits of formal democracy. And only political pedants who do not take into account the revolutionary logic of class relations can, in the face of the post-October situation, deliver futile lectures to the proletariat on the benefits and advantages of democracy for the cause of the class struggle." "Revolutionary logic" means that revolution of a minority against a majority is required by dialectical logic. In terms of nondialectic logic, a minority cannot come into power in a democratic way. And this is exactly what Trotsky admits in declaring: "The real kernel of the class revolution has come into irreconcilable conflict with its democratic shell."[14] Even more directly Radek declares: "The Soviet Government is no democracy, it is the form of the government of the workers." "Democracy is the domination by capital ... a side-scene (Kulisse) of the domination by capital.[15]

REINTERPRETATION OF THE CONCEPT OF DEMOCRACY
DEMOCRACY IN A CAPITALIST SOCIETY?

In contradistinction to these writers, Lenin, who aspired to be not only a political leader but also an orthodox Marxist, maintained the doctrine of his master that the transformation of the proletariat into the ruling class is identical with the establishment of democracy. Since, however, this dogma was in open contradiction

---

[13] *Ibid.*, p. 80.
[14] *Ibid.*, p. 82.
[15] Radek, *op. cit.*, pp. 29; 26.

to the facts, he was compelled to reinterpret the concept of democracy. In one point, his interpretation of the Marxian doctrine concerning democracy, is certainly correct: "that democracy is also a state and that, consequently, democracy will also disappear when the state disappears."[16] Democracy may be the form of the proletarian state, not of the stateless society of the last phase of communism. But for the state established by the proletarian revolution, Lenin apparently sticks to the Marxian postulate of democracy as a self-evident requirement. He says: "We all know that the political form of the 'state' at that time (after the Revolution) is complete democracy."[17] There are, however, other statements which show that this profession of faith in democracy as the form of government of the proletarian state is not at all unconditional. Thus, Lenin says: "A democratic republic is the best possible political shell for capitalism, and, therefore, once capital has gained control ... of this very best shell, it establishes its power so securely, so firmly that no change, either of persons, or institutions, or parties in the bourgeois republic can shake it."[18] Is this the "democratic republic" of which Engels said that it is only this form of government under which the working class can come to power and at the same time, "the specific form for the dictatorship of the proletariat"? And of which Lenin, in another connection, says that "it is of great importance for the working class in its struggle for freedom against the capitalists."[19] This "democratic republic" is evidently the specific political form of capitalism, and not of the dictatorship of the proletariat—as Radek, Bukharin, and Trotsky more sincerely admitted. If, in accordance with the words of the prophets the dictatorship of the proletariat must be interpreted as a democracy, then the capitalist state—for which the democratic republic is "the best possible political shell"—cannot be a democracy. To prove this, Lenin first admits again that even in capitalist society a "complete democracy" is possible. "In capitalist society, under conditions most favorable to its development, we have more or less complete democracy in the democratic republic."[20] This "more or less complete democracy" is, in reality,

---

[16] *State and Revolution*, p. 17; p. 67.
[17] *Ibid.*, p. 17.
[18] *Ibid.*, p. 14.
[19] *Ibid.*, p. 82.
[20] *Ibid.*, p. 71.

no democracy at all. "But this democracy is always bound by the narrow framework of capitalist exploitation, and consequently always remains, in reality, a democracy for the minority, only for the possessing classes, only for the rich. Freedom in capitalist society always remains just about the same as it was in the ancient Greek republics: freedom for the slave-owners. The modern wage-slaves, owing to the conditions of capitalist exploitation, are so much crushed by want and poverty that 'democracy is nothing to them,' 'politics is nothing to them'; that, in the ordinary peaceful course of events, the majority of the population is debarred from participating in social and political life."[21] This statement is evidently not correct. But its correctness or incorrectness is of no importance here. It is interesting only that Lenin, in this connection, denies that democracy exists in a capitalist state, since there the majority of the population is excluded from participating in political life. Such exclusion is certainly incompatible with democracy.

IDENTIFICATION OF DEMOCRACY WITH SOCIALISM

Lenin justifies his statement by two different arguments. The first is the already mentioned fact of "capitalist exploitation." This fact must be admitted. It concerns the economic content of the state order, not its political form. And, as pointed out, democracy is, in the first place, a specific *form* of the state, not a specific *content* of the state order. That the capitalist system of economy may coexist with the highest possible degree of democracy is a fact which cannot be denied, though its explanation may not be very pleasant to Marxists. It might be said that democracy is of no use if it does not necessarily lead to socialism. But it is an unpermissible confusion of concepts to deny that a state whose constitution fulfills all requirements of democracy as a form of government is a democracy because the economic system of that state is—in spite of its democratic form of government—capitalism, and not socialism.

Besides, if the basic principle of democracy is freedom, not only positive freedom in the sense of active participation of the citizens in the government, but also negative freedom in the sense of certain restrictions of the state power in relation to the individual: freedom of conscience, of speech and press, and of association, that

---

[21] *Ibid.*, pp. 71 ff.

is to say, if political liberalism is considered to be an essential element of democracy, then the economic system of capitalism is much more related to the political system of democracy than is the economic system of socialism. For the basic principle of capitalism is freedom in economic life, economic liberalism, whereas social-ism, as a system of strictly planned economy, operates under a principle directly opposite to economic liberalism. Concerning the ideas at the basis of the respective systems, it would be more plau-sible to assume that only a capitalist state can be a true democracy, than to say that no capitalist, but only a socialist, state can be a true democracy. However, neither the one nor the other statement is correct. The political form of democracy is compatible with a capitalist as well as with a socialist economic system as its content. And the same is true with respect to the political form of autoc-racy. If a dictator, for some reason or other, establishes or main-tains a socialist economic system, his government remains an autocracy and does not assume the character of a democracy. But this is exactly one of the undercurrents in Lenin's argumentation : to let the dictatorship of the proletariat pass as a democracy, not because it fulfills the requirements of that political system as a form of government, but because it establishes socialism. To iden-tify socialism with democracy amounts to the attempt to substitute the one for the other.

IMPORTANCE OF CAPITALIST DEMOCRACY FOR THE STRUGGLE FOR SOCIALISM

It seems that even Lenin himself did not consider very convincing the argument that a state is not a democracy because its economic system is not socialism. For he adds another argument to prove that the capitalist state—for which the "democratic republic is the best possible political shell"—is no democracy at all. This argu-ment refers, indeed, to the form of government.

Democracy for an insignificant minority, democracy for the rich—that is the democracy of capitalist society. If we look more closely into the mechanism of capitalist democracy, everywhere, both in the "petty"—so-called petty—details of the suffrage (residential qualification, exclusion of women, etc.) and in the technique of the representative institutions, in the actual obstacles to the right of assembly ("public buildings are not for beggars"!), in the purely capitalist organization of the daily press, etc., etc.—on all sides we see re-striction after restriction upon democracy. These restrictions, exceptions, exclusions, obstacles for the poor, seem slight, especially in the eyes of one who has himself never known want and has never been in close contact with the oppressed classes in their mass life (and nine-tenths, if not ninety-nine hundredths, of the bourgeois publicists and politicians are of this class) but in their sum total these restrictions exclude and squeeze out the poor from politics and from an active share in democracy.[22]

These statements are partly in open contradiction to the facts, partly gross exaggerations. In most of the capitalist democracies, women are not excluded from suffrage, and the "residential qualifications" have, as a rule, no decisive effect on the outcome of the elections. The statement that "public buildings are not for beggars" can hardly be taken as a serious criticism of any of the existing democracies; and it is certainly impossible to speak of a "purely" capitalist organization of the press in view of the undeniable fact that in all capitalist democracies there exist—owing to the freedom of press—socialist newspapers which sometimes have remarkable political influence. If the spread of these papers is sometimes not so large as that of bourgeois papers it is certainly not because of any "oppression." It is, however, superfluous to reject all these statements, for Lenin does it himself, in admitting that democracy—the democracy of the capitalist state—"is of great importance for the working class in its struggle for freedom against the capitalists." This fact would not be true, if within such a pseudodemocracy the majority of the people "were debarred from participating in political life," if the restrictions working in the mechanism of capitalist democracy could "exclude and squeeze out the poor from politics and from an active share in democracy."

DICTATORSHIP OF THE PROLETARIAT: A TRUE DEMOCRACY?

According to Lenin, the capitalist state is not a true democracy because of certain restrictions—which in truth do not exist or are of no decisive importance; but the dictatorship of the proletariat is a true, a complete democracy in spite of much more incisive restrictions, openly admitted by Lenin as necessary and essential to such dictatorship. Lenin declares that from the capitalist democracy "inevitably narrow, subtly rejecting the poor, and therefore hypocritical and false to the core, progress does not march onward, simply, smoothly and directly, to 'greater and greater democracy' as the liberal professors and petty-bourgeois oppor-

[22] *Ibid.*, p. 72.

tunists would have us believe."[23] A revolution is necessary to establish the dictatorship of the proletariat. "But the dictatorship of the proletariat—i.e., the organization of the vanguard of the oppressed as the ruling class for the purpose of crushing the oppressors—cannot produce merely an expansion of democracy." But such expansion of democracy is the effect of the dictatorship of the proletariat. However, there are, on the other hand, "restrictions." "Together with an immense expansion of democracy which for the first time becomes democracy for the poor, democracy for the people, and not democracy for the rich folk, the dictatorship of the proletariat produces a series of restrictions of liberty in the case of the oppressors, the exploiters, the capitalists. We must crush them in order to free humanity from wage-slavery; their resistance must be broken by force." This notion is hardly compatible with democracy, especially not with an "immense expansion of democracy." And in open contradiction to his statement that the political form of the state established by the proletarian revolution is the "most complete democracy," Lenin frankly admits in this connection: "It is clear that where there is suppression, there is also violence, there is no liberty, no democracy."[24] "Immense expansion of democracy" exists on the one hand, but on the other hand there is no democracy at all, because there is "violent suppression of one group by the other." But in another context, Lenin says: "Democracy is a state recognizing the subordination of the minority to the majority, i.e., an organization for the systematic use of violence by one class against the other, by one part of the population against another."[25] In accordance with this definition, the dictatorship of the proletariat is a true democracy just because it is the systematical use of violence by one class for the suppression of another class, that is to say, in the sense of the Marxian doctrine, a "state." But, says Lenin in the first chapter of his *State and Revolution,* no state can be a true democracy for "every state is a 'special repressive force' for the suppression of the oppressed class. Consequently, no state is either 'free' or a 'people's' state."[26] "People's free state" was a demand in the program of the German Social Democrats; "this slogan," says Lenin, is nothing but "a pompous middle-class circumlocution of the idea of democracy."[27] In consequence of the doctrine that no state can

---

[23] *Ibid.,* p. 73.   [25] *Ibid.,* p. 68.   [27] *Ibid.,* p. 18.
[24] *Ibid.*   [26] *Ibid.,* p. 16 f.

be a democracy—a doctrine advocated in contradiction to the doctrine likewise advocated that only a state can be a democracy and that democracy is for the working class the best form of government in a capitalist state and, at the same time, the form of government of the proletarian state—Lenin declares: "Only in [a] communist society, when the resistance of the capitalists has been completely broken, when the capitalists have disappeared, when there are no classes (i.e., there is no difference between the members of society in their relation to the social means of production), only then 'the state ceases to exist,' and 'it becomes possible to speak of freedom.' Only then a really full democracy, a democracy without any exceptions, will be possible and will be realized."[28] First, the "most complete democracy" was the proletarian state, and democracy is possible only within a state. Now, "full democracy" is possible only when this state has ceased to exist. But this "full democracy" "will be realized" only in order to disappear. Lenin continues: "Only then will democracy itself begin to wither away." After the state has ceased to exist, democracy will only "begin" to wither away, so that there will be a period during which the communist society will be no state but still a democracy, in spite of the fact—upon which Lenin insisted in another connection—that "democracy is also a state" and "consequently democracy will also disappear when the state disappears."

All these absurd contradictions are the inevitable consequence of the fact that the dictatorship of the proletariat is just what it calls itself: a dictatorship, not a democracy, and the fact that it must be interpreted to be democracy, since it is called so by Marx and Engels. If used or misused in this way, the term "democracy" must lose any specific meaning. To what extent such misuse is possible is shown by a statement Lenin made in his speech on "Economic Construction," March 31, 1920: "Now we are drawn back to a question that was decided long ago, in a manner approved of and made clear by the Central Executive Committee—namely that the Soviet Socialist Democracy is in no way inconsistent with the rule and dictatorship of one person; that the will of a class is at times best realized by a dictator, who sometimes will accomplish more by himself and is frequently more needed."[29]

---

[28] *Ibid.*, p. 78.
[29] Lenin, *Selected Works* (1st Russian ed.); Vol. XVII, p. 89; quoted in J. Martov, *The State and the Socialist Revolution* (New York, 1938), p. 31.

DICTATORSHIP OF THE PROLETARIAT : DICTATORSHIP OF THE COMMUNIST PARTY

If the question of the form of government of the Soviet state is to be answered on the basis of its real constitution, and not in accordance with the Holy Scriptures of Communism, it becomes even more evident that the first state established by a socialist revolution represents a typical case of a dictatorship of a political party which brings Bolshevik Russia into the same category with Nazi Germany and Fascist Italy. It can hardly be denied that the so-called dictatorship of the proletariat in Russia was from the very beginning the dictatorship of the Bolshevik party. In a discussion at the Second Congress of the Communist International, Lenin made the following statement:

Tanner says that he stands for the dictatorship of the proletariat, but that he pictures the dictatorship of the proletariat to be something different from what we do. He says that by the dictatorship of the proletariat we mean, in essence, the dictatorship of its organized and class conscious minority. And as a matter of fact, in the era of capitalism, when the masses of the workers are constantly subjected to exploitation and cannot develop their human faculties, the most characteristic feature of working class political parties is that they can embrace only a minority of their class. A political party can organize only a minority of the class, in the same way as the really class conscious workers in every capitalist society comprise only a minority of all the workers. That is why we must admit that only this class conscious minority can guide the broad masses of the workers and lead them. And if Comrade Tanner says that he is opposed to parties, and at the same time is in favour of the minority, representing the best organized and the most revolutionary workers, showing the way to the whole of the proletariat, then I say that there is really no difference between us.[30]

The "minority representing the best organized and the most revolutionary workers" is the Communist party. Dictatorship by this minority is dictatorship by the Communist party. Its existence is here admitted by Lenin.

STALIN'S INTERPRETATION OF "DICTATORSHIP"

Stalin tries to obliterate Lenin's admission that there exists a party dictatorship in Soviet Russia. His interpretation of Lenin's view is laid down in the following statement:

---

[30] Lenin, *Selected Works* (Russian ed.), Vol. X, p. 214; quoted in Stalin, *Leninism* (London, 1942), p. 135.

(a) Lenin did not regard the formula "the dictatorship of the Party" as being irreproachable and exact, for which reason it is very rarely used in Lenin's works, and is sometimes put in quotation marks. (b) On the few occasions that Lenin was obliged, in controversy with opponents, to speak of the dictatorship of the Party, he usually referred to the "dictatorship of *one* party," i.e., to the fact that our Party holds power *alone*, that it *does not share* power with *other* parties. Moreover, he always made it clear that the dictatorship of the Party *in relation to the working class* meant the leadership of the Party, its leading role. (c) In all those cases in which Lenin found it necessary to give a scientific definition of the role of the Party in the system of the dictatorship of the proletariat, he spoke *exclusively* of the leading role of the Party in relation to the working class (and there were thousands of such cases). (d) That was why it "never occurred" to Lenin to include the formula "dictatorship of the Party" in the fundamental resolution on the role of the Party (I have in mind the resolution adopted at the Second Congress of the Communist International). (e) Those comrades who identify, or try to identify the "dictatorship" of the Party, and consequently, the "dictatorship of the leaders," with the dictatorship of the proletariat are wrong from the point of view of Leninism, and are politically short-sighted, for they thereby violate the conditions of the correct relations between the vanguard and the class."[31]

The decisive argument against the correctness of the term "dictatorship of the Party," according to Stalin, is that it "incorrectly attributes to the Party, the function of employing violence against the working class as a whole."[32] That the Communist party does not employ violence against the working class as a whole is certainly true. But this does not exclude the undeniable fact that the Communist party employs violence against all individual members of the working class who do not follow the Communist party line. This fact, together with the exclusion of all other parties, perfectly justifies the use of the term "party dictatorship."

THE CONSTITUTION OF 1936

The fact of party dictatorship cannot be veiled even by the new Constitution of 1936, the so-called Stalin Constitution, by which most of the restrictions on the political rights of the citizens established by the previous constitutions of 1918 and 1924 have been set aside. The abolishment of these restrictions is justified by the fact that the new constitution—according to the testimony of Stalin himself—proceeds from the presupposition "that there are no

[31] Stalin, *Leninism*, p. 151.
[32] *Ibid.*, p. 139.

longer any antagonistic classes in society, that society consists of two friendly classes, of workers and peasants, that it is these classes, the toiling classes, that are in power, that the guidance of society by the state (the dictatorship) is in the hands of the working class, the most advanced class in society, that a constitution is needed for the purpose of consolidation of a social order desired by and beneficial to the toilers."[33] These statements mean that the Soviet state is no longer "an instrument in the hands of the ruling class for suppressing the resistance of the class enemies," no longer a dictatorship of the proletariat, since there is no longer any proletariat to exercise such dictatorship, nor any bourgeoisie to be suppressed. Such a state has certainly no reason not to be a full democracy. And it seems, at first sight, that the Constitution of 1936 was intended to establish such a democracy. It is perfectly true, as Stalin said, that the constitution is "free from such reservations and limitations" as other constitutions maintain, that for the new Soviet constitution "active and passive citizens do not exist; for it, all citizens are active. It does not recognize any difference in rights as between men and women, 'residence' and 'nonresidence,' propertied and propertyless, educated and uneducated. For it, all citizens have equal rights. It is not property status, not national origin, not sex, not office that determines the position of every citizen in society, but personal ability and personal labor." The legislative and executive organs of the Soviet state are elected by the people on the basis of an electoral system which is perfectly democratic. A Bill of Rights guarantees the citizens freedom of speech, freedom of press, freedom of assemblies and meetings, freedom of street processions and demonstrations, and the "right of union into public organizations, professional unions, coöperative organizations, organizations of youth, sport and defense organizations, cultural, technical and scientific societies"; further, inviolability of persons and of residence, and secrecy of correspondence.

The Soviet Constitution fulfills all requirements of a radical democracy, except one: there is no freedom of formation and activity of political parties. Only one political party, the Communist party, is legally permitted, and no candidate can be elected who is not approved by this party. The written constitution, it is true, does not forbid other parties. It says of the Communist party

---

[33] Stalin, *Leninism, Selected Writings* (New York, 1942), p. 388.

only that "the most active and conscious citizens from the ranks
of the working class and other strata of toilers are united in the
All-Union Communist Party (Bolsheviks) which is the vanguard
of the toilers in their struggle for the strengthening and development of the socialist order and represents the directing kernel of
all organizations of toilers, both public and State." (Art. 126.)
The last statement may be interpreted to mean that all organizations are placed under the political control of the Communist
party. This is certainly the actual situation in Soviet Russia. It
is in the light of this fact that the provision of the Constitution
must be understood that "the right of nomination of candidates
(for the elections) is ensured to public organizations and societies
of toilers; Communist Party organizations, professional unions,
coöperatives, organizations of youth, cultural societies." (Art.
141.)

POLITICAL REALITY IN SOVIET RUSSIA

In reality, the Communist party has exclusive and absolute control of the nomination of candidates. As a rule only one candidate
is submitted to the voters in each electoral district, so that no
public contest actually takes place and the voters have only a
choice between approving or not approving (by a blank ballot)
the candidate—directly or indirectly—presented by the ruling
party. In the elections of 1937 and 1938, 98.6 per cent of the
electors voted for the candidates. In the general elections in 1946
also, the voters could ballot for only one candidate for each position who had been nominated in advance. It is significant that in
this election campaign the President of the Soviet Union, N. I.
Kalinin, thought it necessary to justify this electoral system by
which any competition between candidates representing different
political programs is excluded. He said that in bourgeois democracies the elections are contests for power between political parties
that are "not calculated to rouse and develop the political mind
of the masses, but to deaden and blind them and crush the slightest
sign of independent political thought." In the Soviet Union, the
elections, according to President Kalinin, are more like reviews of
the state of the nation. "The business qualities and political value
of the candidates are discussed and their previous activities evalu-
ated. As a result, by polling day the electors have unanimously
chosen a definite person who answers the requirements, for whom

they will cast their votes unanimously."[84] In the election of 1946 most of the candidates were members of the Communist party; but some nonparty members were nominated too. In his speech on the eve of these elections (February 9, 1946) Stalin said, after a report on the activity of the Communist party, "I consider that the election campaign is the judgment of the electors on the Communist Party as being the party of the rulers. The result of the elections will signify the verdict of the electors. Our party would not be worth much if it were afraid to face this verdict. The Communist Party is not afraid to receive the verdict of the electors."[85] In view of the fact that the voters had no real choice, there could be no doubt about this "verdict." As a matter of fact 99.18 per cent of the total number of electors who came to the polls, voted for the candidates of the block of Communists and nonparty people; only 0.81 per cent opposed the nominees.[86] In this speech, Stalin also justified the Communist party entering the elections together with nonparty members. "In former days Communists had an attitude of a certain mistrust towards non-party persons." But "now times have changed. Non-party people are now separated from the bourgeoisie by a barrier which is called the Soviet social system. This very same barrier unites the non-party people with the Communists into one common collective of Soviet peoples ... The sole difference between them is that some of them are members of the party and others are not. But this difference is only a formal one." It is all the more a "formal one," since no nonparty member can be nominated against the will of the party.

Nothing is more characteristic of the fact that political life in Soviet Russia is under the complete dictatorship of the Communist party than that the deputies thus elected—party or nonparty people—the members of the Supreme Council of the U.S.S.R., adopt all decisions by unanimous vote. The Soviet Constitution of 1936 is a splendid democratic façade behind which a relatively small group of men exercise unrestricted control over one of the greatest nations of the world.

In his report on the draft Constitution, Stalin frankly admits that this constitution does not grant "freedom to political parties,"

---

[84] New York *Times*, February 8, 1946, p. 4.
[85] *Ibid.*, February 10, 1946, p. 30.
[86] *Information Bulletin of the Embassy of the U.S.S.R.*, Washington, D.C., Vol. VI, No. 24 (1946), p. 5.

but "preserves unchanged the present leading position of the Communist Party of the U.S.S.R." He even makes an attempt to justify the one-party system as democratic.

A party is a part of a class, its most advanced part. Several parties, and, consequently, freedom for parties, can exist only in a society in which there are antagonistic classes whose interests are mutually hostile and irreconcilable—in which there are, say, capitalists and workers, landlords and peasants, kulaks and poor peasants, etc. But in the U.S.S.R. there are no longer such classes as the capitalists, the landlords, the kulaks, etc. In the U.S.S.R. there are only two classes, workers and peasants, whose interests—far from being mutually hostile—are, on the contrary, friendly. Hence there is no ground in the U.S.S.R. for the existence of several parties, and, consequently, for freedom for these parties. In the U.S.S.R. there is ground only for one party, the Communist Party. In the U.S.S.R. only one party can exist, the Communist Party, which courageously defends the interests of the workers and peasants to the very end.[37]

If a political party were really nothing but "a part of a class," and if more than one party could only exist where antagonistic classes exist, there would be no reason not to grant complete freedom to political parties in Soviet Russia. For, since no antagonistic classes exist there, only one political party could come into existence. However, the history of Soviet Russia shows clearly: first, that even at a time when there still existed antagonistic classes, "capitalists and workers, landlords and peasants, kulaks and poor peasants," only one party, the Communist party, was permitted; and, second, that within one and the same class, two antagonistic political parties may be formed. If the Soviet State does not "wither away," in spite of the fact that there is no longer a bourgeois class to suppress, it is certainly also because there may still be political parties, antagonistic to the Communist party, to be suppressed. In spite of the fact that there are no antagonistic classes in Soviet Russia, there is nevertheless a great danger of the appearance of political parties hostile to the ruling party. And because formation and activity of such parties must be prevented, the Soviet state is no democracy. But this does not prevent Stalin from declaring, after having admitted the existence of the "leadership of the Communist Party" and the exclusion of all other political parties—which means the dictatorship of the Com-

---

[37] Stalin, *Leninism, Selected Writings*, p. 395.

munist party—"that the Constitution of the U.S.S.R. is the only thoroughly democratic constitution in the World."

It is strange that the Bolshevik theory as the ideology of a true revolutionary movement which openly admits its intention of destroying by violence all values, the sham values, of the past in order to build up a new and better world, that this doctrine as presented by its most outstanding authority in open contradiction to the facts, and at the price of highly problematic distortions, pretends to spare just one value of a doomed civilization : the ideal of democracy. This *sacrificium intellectus* may be explained by the fact that even the most revolutionary philosophy of life cannot ignore man's indestructible desire for freedom, which, if it cannot be satisfied by deeds must be satisfied at least by words. That the Bolshevik doctrine tries to make us believe that democracy is the only value to be taken over from the old capitalist to the new communist society may, in addition, be explained even better by the extraordinary advantage a democratic terminology has in a political struggle which, although not primarily nor exclusively, is nevertheless directed against democracy.

SELECTED BIBLIOGRAPHY

BUKHARIN, NIKOLAI, *The Communist Program.* New York, 1920.

———, *Historical Materialism.* New York, 1925.

Blueprint for World Conquest, as Outlined by the Communist International. With an Introduction by William Henry Chamberlin. Washington, D.C., and Chicago, 1946.

COKER, F. W., *Recent Political Thought.* New York, 1934.

ENGELS, FRIEDRICH, *Herr Eugen Dühring's Revolution in Science [Anti-Dühring].* New York, 1939.

———, *The Origin of the Family, Private Property and the State.* Marxist Library, Vol. XXII. New York, 1942.

KAUTSKY, KARL, *The Dictatorship of the Proletariat.* Manchester, 1920.

LASKI, HAROLD J., *Communism.* London, 1937.

LENIN, V. I., *State and Revolution.* Little Lenin Library, vol. 14, New York, 1935.

MARTOV, J., *The State and the Socialist Revolution.* New York, 1928.

MARX, KARL, and FRIEDRICH ENGELS, *The Communist Manifesto.* London, 1930.

OAKESHOTT, MICHAEL, *The Social and Political Doctrines of Contemporary Europe.* New York, 1942.

SOMERVILLE, JOHN, *Soviet Philosophy.* New York, 1946.

STALIN, JOSEPH, *Leninism.* London, 1942.

———, *Problems of Leninism.* Marxist Library, Vol. XXXII. New York, 1934.

TROTSKY, LEON, *From October to Brest-Litowsk.* New York, 1919.

WEBB, SIDNEY and BEATRICE, *Soviet Communism. A New Civilization?* New York, 1938.

BY THE SAME AUTHOR

General Theory of Law and State, 2d printing, Cambridge, Harvard University Press, 1946.

Law and Peace in International Relations, 2d printing, Cambridge, Harvard University Press, 1948.

Society and Nature. A Sociological Inquiry, Chicago, University of Chicago Press, 1943.

Peace Through Law, Chapel Hill, University of North Carolina Press, 1944.

Hans Kelsen

Titles published by
The Lawbook Exchange, Ltd.

Possibly the most influential jurisprudent of the twentieth century, Hans Kelsen [1881-1973] was legal adviser to Austria's last emperor and its first republican government, the founder and permanent advisor of the Supreme Constitutional Court of Austria, and the author of Austria's Constitution, which was enacted in 1920, abolished during the Anschluss, and restored in 1945. He was the author of more than forty books on law and legal philosophy.

Active as a teacher in Europe and the United States, he was Dean of the Law Faculty of the University of Vienna and taught at the universities of Cologne and Prague, the Institute of International Studies in Geneva, Harvard, Wellesley, the University of California at Berkeley, and the Naval War College.

Collective Security Under International Law

Washington, D.C.: United States Government Printing Office, 1957
vi, 275 pp.

Hardcover 2001
ISBN 9781584771449
$75.

The noted jurist Hans Kelsen advances his theory that collective security is "...an essential function of law, national as well as international, and that, therefore, there exists an intrinsic connection between international security and international law; in other terms, that collective security of the state is, just as collective security of the individual within the state, by its very nature a legal problem." Foreword p. ii.

General Theory of Law and State

Translated by Anders Wedberg
Cambridge: Harvard University Press, 1945
xxxiii, 516 pp.

Hardcover 1999
ISBN 9781886363748
$95.

Paperback 2007
ISBN 9781584777175
$29.95

Reprint of the first edition. This classic work by the important Austrian jurist is the fullest exposition of his enormously influential pure theory of law, which includes a theory of the state. It also has an extensive appendix that discusses the pure theory in comparison with the law of nature, positivism, historical natural law, metaphysical dualism and scientific-critical philosophy.

> The scope of the work is truly universal. It never loses itself in vague generalities or in unconnected fragments of thought. On the contrary, precision in the formulation of details and rigorous system are characteristic features of the exposition: only a mind fully concentrated upon that logical structure can possibly follow Kelsen's penetrating analysis. Such a mind will not shrink from the effort necessary for acquainting itself with...the pure theory of law in its more general aspects, and will then pass over to the theory of the state which ends up with a carefully worked out theory of international law.
>
> Julius Kraft,
> *American Journal of International Law* 40 (1946):496

The Law of the United Nations
A Critical Analysis of Its
Fundamental Problems

New York: Frederick A. Praeger, [1964]
xvii, 994 pp.

Hardcover 2000
ISBN 9781584770770
$150.

First published under the auspices of The London Institute of World Affairs in 1950. With a supplement, *Recent Trends in the Law of the United Nations* [1951]. A critical, detailed, highly technical legal analysis of the United Nations charter and organization.

Peace Through Law

Chapel Hill: The University of North CarolinaPress, 1944
xii, 155 pp.

Hardcover 2008
ISBN 9781584771036
$60.

Paperback 2008
ISBN 9781584779209
$24.95

Reprint of the only edition. Kelsen departs from his theories on pure law and here proposes a formula for international peace. He proffers "peace guaranteed by compulsory adjudication of international disputes," (Part I): the formation of a world court with the authority to resolve international conflicts, and "peace guaranteed by individual responsibility for violations of international law," (Part II): that individual statesmen take personal moral and legal responsibility for war crimes and other acts of violation committed by their country.

Principles of International Law

New York: Rinehart & Company, Inc. [1952]
xvii, 461 pp.

Hardcover 2003
ISBN 9781584773252
$85.

Upon his retirement from the faculty of the University of California at Berkeley in 1952, noted legal philosopher and political scientist Hans Kelsen produced arguably this his most important work.

> ... a systematic study of the most important aspects of international law, including international delicts and sanctions, reprisals, the spheres of validity and the essential function of international law, creation and application of international law and national law.
>
> Nicoletta Bersier Ladavac,
> "Hans Kelsen (1881 - 1973) Biographical Note and Bibliography,"
> *European Journal of International Law* Vol. 9 (1998) No. 2

Pure Theory of Law

Translation from the Second German Edition
by Max Knight

Berkeley: University of California Press, 1967
x, 356 pp.

Hardcover 2002, 2009
ISBN 9781584772064
$95.

Paperback 2005
ISBN 9781584775782
$36.95

Second revised and enlarged edition, a complete revision of the first edition published in 1934. A landmark in the development of modern jurisprudence, the pure theory of law defines law as a system of coercive norms created by the state that rests on the validity of a generally accepted Grundnorm, or basic norm, such as the supremacy of the Constitution. Entirely self-supporting, it rejects any concept derived from metaphysics, politics, ethics, sociology, or the natural sciences.

Beginning with the medieval reception of Roman law, traditional jurisprudence has maintained a dual system of "subjective" law (the rights of a person) and "objective" law (the system of norms). Throughout history this dualism has been a useful tool for putting the law in the service of politics, especially by rulers or dominant political parties. The pure theory of law destroys this dualism by replacing it with a unitary system of objective positive law that is insulated from political manipulation.

Society and Nature
A Sociological Inquiry

London: K. Kegan Paul, Trench, Trubner & Co., Ltd., [1946]
viii, 391 pp.

Hardcover 2000
ISBN 9781584770640
$85.

Paperback 2009
ISBN 9781584779865
$65.

This interesting work offers a sociological and ethno-graphic perspective on Kelsen's juristic thinking. His central thesis, which ranges over the history of human-ity, argues that the idea of causality developed from primitive ideas of retribution. He shows how early man developed his interpretation of nature through the laws of retribution and causality, then developed our cur-rent concept of nature and society over time. He holds that the gradual emancipation of the law of causality from the principle of retribution is "the emancipation from a social interpretation of nature," a process "very important from the point of view of intellectual history." (Introduction viii). *Society and Nature* was originally published in 1943 to mixed reviews. It deserves a fresh appraisal for its original ideas and insights into Kelsen's theory of pure positive law outlined in *Pure Theory of Law* and *General Theory of Law and State*.

What is Justice?
Justice, Law and Politics in the Mirror of Science

Berkeley: University of California Press, 1957
[vi], 397 pp.

Hardcover 2000
ISBN 9781584771012
$95.

Through the lens of science, Kelsen proposes a dynamic theory of natural law, examines Platonic and Aristotelian doctrines of justice, the idea of justice as found in the holy scriptures, and defines justice as "...that social order under whose protection the search for truth can prosper. 'My' justice, then, is the justice of freedom, the justice of peace, the justice of democracy-the justice of tolerance." (p. 24).

www.ingramcontent.com/pod-product-compliance
Lightning Source LLC
Chambersburg PA
CBHW020709270326
41928CB00005B/343